Contents

Acknowledgements

Allen Memorial Art Museum, Oberlin College: 6. Ashmolean Museum: 4. Aspect (photo: Pierre Jaunet): 55. Chris Barker (Courtesy Boleskine House Collection): 121. G. P. & J. Barker Ltd: 126. Trustees of the British Museum: 79, 86, 87, 96BR, 113 (photo: R. B. Fleming), 114 (photo: Jerry Tubby). C. A. Burland (Museo de America): 104. Marie Caboue: 65. Courtesy of the Art Institute of Chicago: 15. Bruce Coleman: 49BR. Courtauld Institute Galleries, London: 33. Alan Duns: 128. Escher Foundation, Gemeentemuseum, The Hague: 116. Giraudon: 10 (Lehmann Coll. New York), 18, 36 (Musée Municipal, Grenoble), 38, 72 (Cabinet des Dessins, Louvre), 88 (Musée Municipal, Cambrai), 96TL, 115B (Bibliothèque National, Paris), 122 (Musée Lazaro Galdiano, Madrid). Melvyn Grey: 51, 52. Hamburger Kunsthalle: 84. Harrison Artistic Enterprises, Birmingham: 26. Hartley Reece & Company (Rotring): 17. William Heineham Ltd: 118. Reproduced with permission of the controller of Her Majesty's Stationery Office: 1, 2. Hunterian Art Gallery, University of Glasgow, Mackintosh Coll. 109. Jeu de Paume, Paris: 5BR. David Kelly: 32. Courtesy of Knoedler Gallery, London: 11, 37. Neil Lorimer: 124. Frederico Arborio Mella: 115TR. The Metropolitan Museum of Art, New York: 46, 80TL. Peter Meyers: 7. The Minneapolis Institute of Arts: 59. David Moore: 49BL. Courtesy of the Trustees, National Gallery, London: 63. National Gallery of Art, Washington D.C. Rosenwald Coll: 48. National Museum, Vincent Van Gogh, Amsterdam: 60. National Portrait Gallery, London: 14. Patrimoine des Musée Royeaux des Beaux-Arts, Brussels: 64. Philadelphia Museum of Art: 47. Photo Meyer: 40. Picturepoint (Galleria Nazionale, Oslo): 41. G. R. Roberts: 49TR. William Robinson: 3. Sächsische Landesbibliothek, Dresden: 57. Robert & Lisa Sainsbury Coll. University of East Anglia: 44. Scala: 13 & 70 (Gabinetto Disegni, Uffizi, Firenze) 80TR, 106 (Institute of Art, Siena). Stedelijk Museum, Amsterdam: 117. The Tate Gallery, London: 27, 99. Rodney Todd-White: 61, 97. Turin Royal Library: 43. Victoria & Albert Museum, Crown Copyright: 34, 61 (Rodney Todd-White) 89, 107 (Michael Holford). Malkolm Warrington: 1 (H.M.S.O.), 21 (Cowling & Wilcox), 22/3, 42, 68/9 (The New Neal Street Shop), 102/3 (artists note books: TL. Kate Wickham, BL David Gordon, M. Steven Mantej, BR. Jane McDonald). Royal Windsor Coll. Reproduced by Gracious permission of Her Majesty Queen Elizabeth II: 5TL, 95, 112. Joseph Ziolo: 98 (Robert Laffont). Copyright: "(c) by A.D.A.G.P. Paris 1979": 34, 44. "(c) by S.P.A.D.E.M. Paris 1979": 6, 10, 15, 46, 47, 65, 84, 88, 96TL 115.

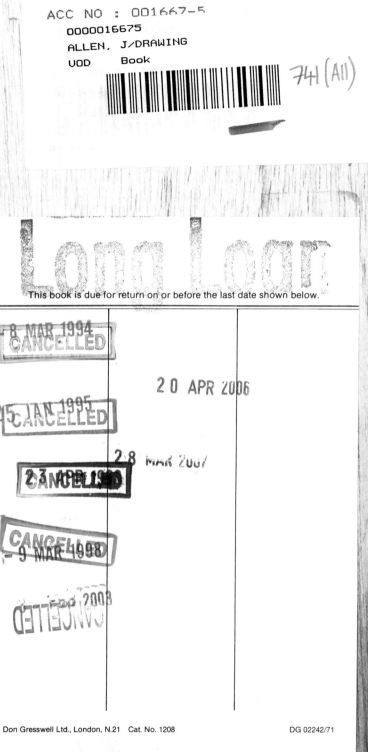

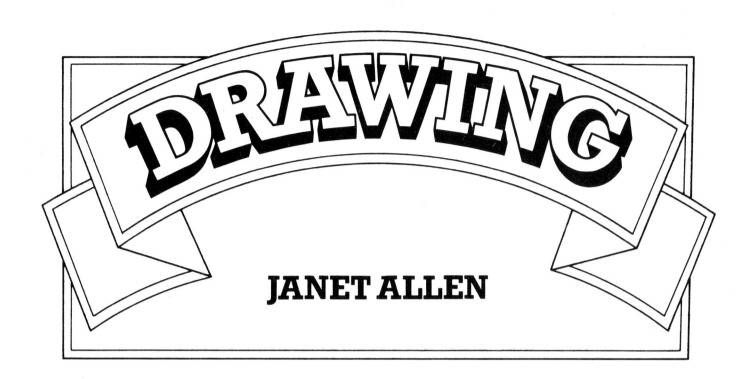

DRAWING

JANET ALLEN

OMEGA BOOKS

A Introduction

Any skill, be it an art, a craft or a sport, has a basic discipline—a set of guidelines. This applies to drawing too. The basics of drawing are examined here and shown not to be tedious, dreary rules, but the very foundations upon which your own personal drawing ability can develop. The different elements that constitute a drawing are explained and projects are suggested for you specifically to explore each of the elements and combinations of them.

Throughout the book drawings by artists of widely differing ages, experience and background are reproduced. Leonardo da Vinci, genius of the fifteenth century, appears alongside a first year art school student of the present day. We can, by all means, all learn and benefit by studying the drawings of the great masters. But their very appellation means that

The sketchbooks of John Constable are an excellent example of how an artist records his visual impressions for later use in a finished composition.

A warning road sign such as this is a fine example of how a drawing uses the most relevant details of a subject to convey a visual message quickly.

they are masters of the drawing art, highly skilled, highly advanced. You can often identify with and, therefore, glean useful help from seeing how someone nearer to your own stage of development has tackled problems very similar to those in which you yourself are at present involved.

What is the most straightforward way of conveying an idea to another person? To show him something. A picture of that thing conveys the idea without the need of that sophisticated device: language. A picture, a representation in two dimensions of something in the real three-dimensional world is universally understood.

Drawing is the most direct way of putting down ideas visually, and it is widely used as a note-making facility to record impressions of a scene or event to be developed later. Drawing is acknowledged as being the basis of all the visual arts.

Drawings are made for many, many reasons. Every artist, quite naturally, discriminates, selects and includes in his drawing those things which are relevant to its purpose. A warning road sign, showing a finely detailed rendering in eye-deceiving 3D of a cliff and a lump of rock falling from it, would leave the passing motorist confused and possibly buried under a heap of rubble—still trying to puzzle out just what that sign meant. Here immediate clarity is all important. What, in real life, is a very complex sight, must be simplified into a visual symbol that can instantly be understood. Conversely, the builder is not going to thank the architect who thought that, for artistic effect on his plans, it would be rather nice to fill in the whole of the south-facing side of a house in solid black.

Not only does the purpose for which the drawing is intended influence and shape its appearance, the 'handwriting' of the artist affects it too. No two people actually write in the same way. We settle down in school, at a tender age, to copy—in fact we are drawing—the shapes of the letters of the alphabet. Every single child will render them differently. By the time we are adult our handwriting styles, because of further outside influences, are diverse. It is just the same with drawing. Everyone, without trying, has his or her own style. So don't try to draw in the manner of somebody else. By all means study the techniques that others use but simply as a 'technical' study. When you then try out a particular kind of pen or pastel your style will come through anyway. Don't even think about cultivating a style; you've got one anyway.

Do remember that it is the doing of the drawing that is the important thing, not the end product. The end product will be interesting if interest has been maintained in the doing.

Anyone can take up drawing. It would appear that there are gifted people in the field of the visual arts as there are in music and languages. Perhaps, for some reason, they are especially aware and responsive to things in a visual way. However, such people are few and far between and this certainly doesn't preclude others from studying and enjoying the subject.

Drawing seems to be a natural, automatic way of expressing oneself. All young children, from whatever cultural background, will draw unselfconsciously to convey to others what they think. A child may not arrange the things in his drawing in the way they actually appear. He may, for example, disregard a wall and draw the contents of a house and its rooms, detailing all the objects he knows to be there.

Regrettably, as we get older, we become increasingly concerned about whether or not the drawing looks like the object being portrayed; also, whether it looks like the type of drawing or painting we admire. The gulf between our perception of objects and our ability to represent them on paper widens. This, unfortunately, has a stultifying effect and usually results in the whole idea being abandoned. In so abandoning, not only

The spontaneity of a child's drawing is something that many artists admire as it precludes any laboured use of colour or form. What is seen in the mind's eye is quickly put down in the simplest terms.

do we jettison any attempts to draw, we also often discard the ability to observe—subsequently missing an enormous amount.

With a very few exceptions, the sort of life people in modern society lead means that the skills and pleasures of observing in order to draw are just simply not required. In the majority of jobs, objects—houses, plants, people, cups and saucers—become statistics. They are counted, tabulated, amassed and distributed—but hardly ever looked at. The kind of candid looking, which is observing to understand, as practised by the artist, is rarely required in everyday life. So it becomes irrelevant to existence. People behave rather as if wearing blinkers. They develop a high degree of proficiency in observing within certain strictly limited areas; outside those areas a dense fog persists. A mother, because of both familiarity and necessity, will instantly perceive any change in her child's appearance, an unaccustomed pallor will immediately alarm her. Yet, because it doesn't really matter to her, she won't be able to recall the shape of her brother's car. The railway ticket inspector will be

The Valley Thick with Corn, *Samuel Palmer. In this drawing pen, ink and wash were used to portray the rich texture of a country landscape.*

intimately familiar with every detail of a ticket; but probably won't remember whether or not his neighbour, whom he passes daily, wears glasses.

Anyhow, in spite of what may seem a dismal situation, anyone can learn to draw. The most important prerequisite is an open mind. The basis of learning to draw is learning to observe in a perfectly straight-forward manner. In a way, it's as if you were to return to the childlike state. Of course, that is not possible for an adult, but the suggested projects in this book, which encourage you to look at particular visual aspects of an object, will help you to shed preconceived and irrelevant ideas. They will help you gradually to regain the confidence and enjoyment that the child has. The various projects will actually impose different sets of limits upon you. You will find that working within these limits, juggling around the cards you have been dealt, is infinitely more instructive and stimulating than being presented with the completely overwhelming choice of the entire pack—literally everything.

With drawing, as with any pursuit, to make progress you must work at it. Drawing is actually hard work. Any creative activity involves work. But it is work of an intensely absorbing kind; so different from your normal routine that you will find yourself completely refreshed after a really concentrated drawing session. Should you doubt the seriousness of drawing try, if you ever have the opportunity, to look in on a life drawing class in an art college. Even in a large class the only sound to be heard is the scratching of many pencils on paper. The dedicated air of concentration equals that of any devoted chess player.

Once you've decided to take up drawing, however slow you feel your progress is at the beginning, you will find you have opened a door to a whole new exciting world of visual awareness. You'll never again see things in the same way. You may even feel that previously you didn't see them anyway. Never again will you be bored.

Look at these widely differing drawings. Consider the things being drawn—the subject matter. What do you draw? Anything and everything. There are no do's and don'ts. Look at all the different media that have been used, and see how the obvious delight in the materials comes across. All the styles are different, the materials are different, the cultural backgrounds and times when the drawings were made are different; but they all share the same essential quality—having something to say.

Woman and Child by the Sea, *Pablo Picasso, pencil. An immediate impression of people relaxing and playing on a beach is given through the use of line only.*

A Materials

When you go into an art supply store you are confronted by a bewildering array of tempting-looking tools, materials, papers and boards. Generally there is no explanation of the way in which they are used or what they are used for. This chapter examines the vast range of drawing materials available, detailing their specific characters and discussing the ways in which they may be used.

As with all crafts, personal preference plays a large part. The tools and materials suggested here will give you a basis, enabling you to start work. Then you will have something by which to judge for yourself what you prefer to use. Do you, for instance, love the feel of a soft pencil on a heavily textured grey paper? Or is a sharp black pen line on a crisp white paper more to your taste?

Have a box or tin in which you keep your drawing kit. This means things are less likely to be mislaid (you can even hide the tin itself if you are plagued by borrowers); also, the tools will be protected and consequently will last longer.

Lead pencils
The wooden pencil, that most commonplace of writing and drawing implements, is manufactured with leads in many degrees of hardness and

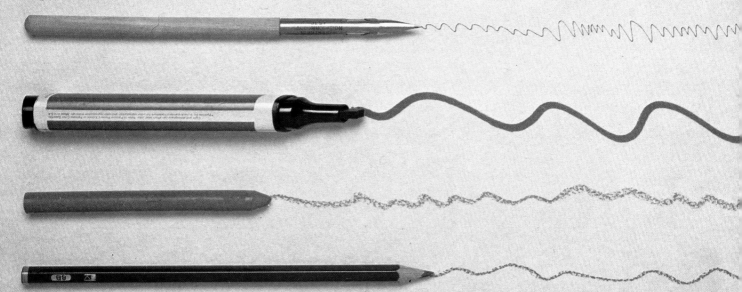

softness. There are also good and poor quality pencils—a fact directly related to their price. The lead in a cheap pencil may be gritty and unpleasant to use, sometimes even failing to make any mark at all. It might also have a tendency to break frequently, so it is worth paying a little extra to buy a reputable brand.

The lead of a pencil does not, in fact, contain any lead. It is a mixture of graphite dust, which makes the black marks, and clay, which carries the graphite dust. This mixture is highly fired so that the clay becomes like glass.

Pencils are graded by the letter H for hard, and B for black or soft. A hard pencil lead contains a high proportion of clay and a small proportion of graphite, so it produces a grey, not very dark, line. In a soft pencil the proportions of clay and graphite are reversed, resulting in a blacker line. Drawing pencils range as follows: 6H, 5H, 4H, 3H, 2H, H, HB, B, 2B, 3B, 4B, 5B, 6B. There are some further grades of pencil manufactured but these are for particular technical purposes, outside the general drawing use.

If possible, try out the pencils in the shop to get the feel of all the different grades before you buy. The HB is a medium, all-purpose pencil so you'll need one of these. The pencils at either extreme of the hardness/softness range are for specialized work. Using a 6H is rather like drawing with a needle, while a 6B gives a thick, broad black mark, inclined to smudge all over the place. Most useful as a start, in addition to an HB, are a 2B and a 2H. The 2B will acquaint you with the delightful responsiveness of a soft pencil, without being so smudgy and black that it gets out of control. Its very responsiveness encourages you to draw freely. The 2H demonstrates how controlled and fine a pencil-drawn line can be.

The type of paper on which you are working has a direct, and very obvious, effect upon the sort of mark your pencil will produce. To use an extreme example, a 6H on cheap shelf paper will simply shred the paper to ribbons. The suggested HB, 2B and 2H pencils will perform adequately on inexpensive drawing paper which is a sensible sort of paper to use for your first drawings.

It is very important to keep your pencil point really sharp, so when you are drawing always keep a craft knife or a sharp penknife handy. To maintain a really good point, every so often rub the lead on the striking edge of a matchbox or on a piece of fine sandpaper. (This is sold in convenient little blocks especially for this purpose.) Pencil sharpeners tend to devour pencils and they don't give such a good point as the knife and sandpaper method. Fig. 1 shows how to sharpen a pencil with a craft knife.

Don't draw with some ancient little pencil stub. Apart from it giving you no pleasure and pride of ownership, a longer pencil will give the

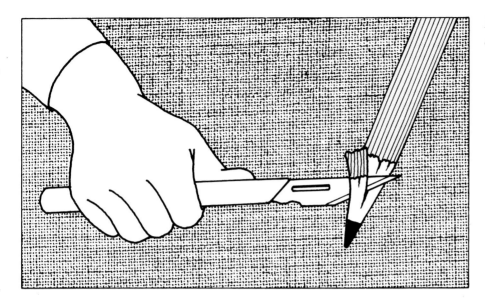

Fig. 1 Sharpening a pencil with a craft knife.

correct balance. The stub would soon make your hand ache.

There are several kinds of leadholders available which will take different grades of pencil or compressed charcoal lead. They are used with fine sandpaper for point sharpening. Rather than going to the expense of buying a leadholder and a selection of leads at the beginning, see first which grades of pencil you prefer. Then invest later if you feel a leadholder will be more convenient than conventional pencils.

When drawing you may find it helpful to keep a piece of plain scrap paper between your work and your drawing hand. This keeps the drawing clean, prevents the pencil lines being smudged and stops grease from your hand getting onto the paper (very relevant on a hot summer's day).

Erasers for pencil drawing

Some people feel that the eraser should be banned. A possible, and understandable, reason for that school of thought is that the nervous beginner will tend to rub out every line as it is drawn, because he or she lacks confidence and feels it must all be wrong. Rather than make yourself neurotic, have a rubber eraser available; but do consider before you employ it. Frequently one rubs out a line because it's felt to be incorrect, only to go and repeat it in exactly the same place. If you think you have drawn something wrongly, re-draw over it. Being able still to see the old incorrect lines will help you to make the new ones more accurate. If you want to, you can erase the mistakes afterwards.

A small, pliable eraser made of rubber or vinyl is suitable for most pencil work. The Blaisdell eraser is shaped like a pencil, the eraser forming the lead. You 'sharpen' it by peeling away a little of the paper strip

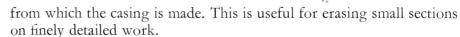

from which the casing is made. This is useful for erasing small sections on finely detailed work.

Certain pencils have a rubber tip—very convenient if you wish to carry as little equipment as possible, as when drawing outdoors. These eraser tips are supplied on a limited range of medium pencil grades, sometimes only on HB.

Charcoal

Charcoal is a most delightful and versatile medium but it does take a little time to become accustomed to it. Don't be discouraged if, at your first attempt, you feel you simply can't cope—all your carefully applied black drawing seems to have transferred from the paper onto you.

The answer to the smudging problem (whereby you're liable instantly to remove an hour's work with one careless sweep of the hand) is to cultivate a delicate touch. Your drawing hand should be held away from the paper. You may find this easier if you stand up to work with your drawing board supported on an easel.

Charcoal is made from carbonized lime, vine or, more commonly, willow twigs. It is available in different sizes, ranging from very thin sticks to thick chunks (scene painter's charcoal). There are soft and hard versions. As you draw it gives off a fine black dust—so don't wear your best clothes. It washes easily off the hands when you have finished work. If you are drawing in a seated position, a good plan is to fix a stiff paper trough along the bottom of the board to prevent you receiving a lap full of fine black powder.

Charcoal can be used for drawing lines—snap a stick to give you a sharp edge for delicate work—or for filling in masses. For the latter either draw repeated lines, or use the charcoal on its side. By varying the amount of pressure you apply you can achieve exceedingly delicate or tentative lines or heavy black masses. It is immensely versatile because of the wide range of light and dark it can encompass.

Wooden pencils are also made with hard and soft charcoal 'leads'. Because of their shape, they obviously produce a more limited range of marks than the conventional, simpler charcoal sticks.

With your finger you can intentionally smudge and smooth together parts of a drawing (you may like to keep a rag handy here). There is also

Below. Study in charcoal of a dancer at rest by Edgar Degas.

the agreeable prospect of being able to work back 'in reverse'—from black to white—by drawing with an eraser. An ordinary eraser will do but the best for any kind of drawing in a soft medium is the kneaded eraser. This is sometimes known as a putty rubber (as it resembles a lump of putty) and it can be moulded with the fingers into a point. You can use it to draw whites or greys into a previously filled-in black area. An alternative, and effective, eraser is a squashed-up piece of soft new white bread.

Coloured pencils

Coloured pencils are made in a similar way to lead pencils, except that pigments replace the graphite. They are produced in very many different

Royal Hawaiian Hotel, Honolulu, 1971, *David Hockney, coloured pencil.*

colours and in various degrees of hardness. Those with a hard 'lead' can be sharpened to a needle point for detailed drawing. These kinds of coloured pencil are non-smudging, so they do not require fixing. A disadvantage, in certain brands, is that the density of colour is rather poor and only pallid colours result, however hard you press. Once again, experiment, if possible, with the pencils before purchasing. Aim for those that are responsive to both a light and a heavier touch. Some brands of coloured pencil can be rubbed out with a pencil eraser.

Water-soluble coloured pencils

Some specially made coloured pencils can be used for a technique that is a mixture of drawing and watercolour painting: you wet the paper with a brush and clean water and draw into it with the pencils; or you can draw on dry paper and then apply water to create washes as you go along. The two methods may be combined.

For the best results use a good quality, somewhat textured paper. Any technique like this that involves dampening the paper and then drawing on it with a sharp instrument demands a tough surface. A poor quality paper would break down and possibly tear.

Wax crayon sticks

There is a wide selection of wax-type stick crayons on the market, varying greatly in size, colour range and brilliance, quality and price. They require no fixing and are very similar to coloured pencils.

Some newly-developed stick crayons are harder than the original wax type, do not melt and can easily be sharpened to a good point. Some may be erased with an ordinary eraser.

Conté crayons

Conté crayon is a French-made refined type of compressed chalk. It is available in square stick form and in wood drawing pencils. There are several natural earth colours, and black and white. Both types of crayon are available in three different degrees of hardness. Conté is an extremely sensitive medium, capable of a wide range of lines and tones. In black it is a little harder and darker than charcoal and less smudgy. It has a special quality all its own. Fixative should be used on a Conté drawing.

The crayon stick may be used on its side to draw a large area of tone. As with charcoal, break the stick to give a sharp drawing end. Both sticks and pencils are rather delicate and they break easily so keep them in some suitable protective packing.

Pastels

Pastel is the drawing medium perhaps most closely allied to painting. The pastel sticks give you the drawing versatility of charcoal—the

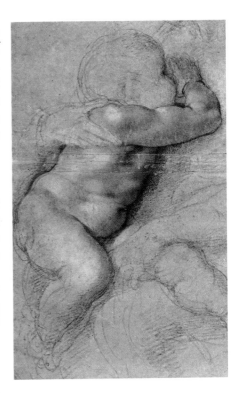

Above. Detail from Madonna and Child, *Michelangelo, chalk.*
Left. Doorway, *Alison Turnbull, pastel.*

*Chalk drawing of Mrs Gaskell,
artist unknown.*

ability to produce delicate lines or to block in solid area—and colour at the same time.

Pastel is a very refined type of coloured chalk. The sticks have a beautiful velvety quality—delectable to use. Artists' pastels are manufactured in soft (exceedingly so), semi-soft and semi-hard grades. There are literally hundreds of colours in some brands, but don't be deterred by this fact. You can buy pastels singly, so initially invest in the basic colours recommended for all media.

Pastel sticks are very fragile so handle them carefully and make sure to keep them in the plastic packing which the shop should supply, if you have no other suitable box. They are, in fact, bound to break. This doesn't matter because you can still use the smaller pieces just as well, but you want to avoid reducing them to dust. In spite of their fragility, pastels are one of the most permanent (least likely to fade or alter) of all the picture-making materials.

There are some pastels available that are harder than the artist's type. They are not so powdery, but in quality they are inferior. Wooden pastel pencils are also on the market. Because of the thinness of the drawing 'lead' the usual scope of the pastel technique is diminished.

The paper trough suggested earlier is also recommended when drawing with pastels. They create a lot of dust which you may occasionally need to blow off your work.

If you need to, use fixative in mid-drawing. Certainly use it when your drawing is completed. All the details given in the charcoal section on fixative and erasers apply equally to pastels.

Chalks

Nowadays the word 'chalk' is generally applied to the material, usually white, which is used so extensively on school blackboards. It is employed in that sense as a drawing material here. Many old masters' works are classified as 'chalk drawings' in museums and in books. This, however, means a drawing medium similar to pastel or Conté. Artists used to make their own drawing and painting materials, to their own individual recipes.

Chalk, of the schoolroom variety, is inferior to pastel in quality and colour choice but it can be used effectively, especially in drawings on a large scale. Go for the softer type, as hard blackboard chalk is not really suitable for use on paper. Chalks are supplied in a very limited range of pale colours. They can be combined most successfully with charcoal. Also, they are extremely cheap. Fixative is essential on a chalk drawing.

Oil pastels and crayons

Oil pastels, which rather resemble sticks of theatrical make-up, are an oil-bound drawing material. Oil crayons are very similar but generally slightly harder. Both are available in a wide range of lovely clear, brilliant colours. They combine a lot of the features of the original type of pastels with those of wax crayons. Neither oil pastels nor crayons require fixing.

Felt and fibre tipped pens and markers

There is a huge choice of felt and fibre tipped pens and markers (which have fatter nibs). They are sold singly or in sets. Some sets contain a

Head of a Woman, *Pablo Picasso, black crayon and gouache.*

vast number of inviting-looking different coloured pens. As they have a somewhat limited life, tending to dry out easily, it may prove more reasonable to choose and buy singly just those colours that you know you need. If you forget to replace their caps the pens will dry up very rapidly.

Some of these pens contain waterproof ink, others are non-waterproof. Ascertain this before you buy, particularly if you intend to use them in a pen and wash drawing as explained in Techniques. The hardness and durability of the nibs vary greatly too. Some of the cheaper brands start life with a nib that draws a clear, precise line. After an alarmingly short time this may well deteriorate into a thing like a chewed stick. The best buy is a refillable felt tipped pen (also made in the larger marker size) which has a range of interchangeable different shaped nibs. Several coloured inks and a cleaner are also available.

No type of felt pen drawing can be erased successfully.

Inks

For the densest black line use waterproof Indian ink. This ink is completely waterproof when dry. It can be diluted when in use, distilled water being recommended. It has, however, a tendency to separate and cannot be successfully stored in a dilute state. Non-waterproof black drawing ink keeps better in dilute form, especially if, again, distilled water is used. Very subtle greys can be achieved for lines or washes.

You can make your own black non-waterproof ink using the ancient method of rubbing a stick of solid Chinese ink in a saucer and gradually adding water. This means that you can control the consistency of the ink—making it paste-like, if you wish—to suit whichever drawing technique you are using. This ink dilutes well.

There is an excellent selection of waterproof coloured drawing inks on the market. These may also be thinned with distilled water. White ink and some metallic colours are available too.

Fountain pen ink is suitable for line drawing and wash work.

Do be sure to wash out your dip pen or brush in clean water after using ink as it stains and clogs badly.

The manufacturers state that the coloured inks are impermanent—they have a tendency to fade.

Pens

Dip pen holders and nibs (the old-fashioned kind) especially intended for drawing are sold in art shops. They differ in the width and pliability of the nib. Varying the pressure applied to the pen when drawing alters the width of the line and, if dilute ink is being used, the tone or darkness of it too. Do not confuse drawing nibs with lettering nibs. The latter are made to give a thin upstroke and a thick downstroke. You can use any kind of ink with a dip pen.

You may find you like to draw with an ordinary writing fountain pen (providing the nib is not too broad), and this eliminates the bother of carrying a bottle of ink around. Use only fountain pen ink as drawing inks will almost certainly clog up the pen.

There are several different brands of barrel fountain pen specifically made for drawing. They have interchangeable nibs in different sizes which produce a clear line of even thickness and constant colour, unlike the dip pen nibs. These are rather expensive, delicate drawing instruments and, for the pen to function properly, you must follow the manufacturer's instructions. Use only the ink and the cleanser that he recommends and don't fiddle with the mechanics—beyond what you are told to do.

Special ink for barrel drawing pens is supplied in a good dense black, and in several colours. All are waterproof.

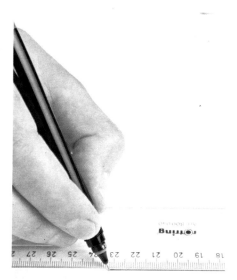

Inset. A barrel fountain pen made specifically for drawing.
Above. This type of pen makes a very clean line and is good for very detailed drawings.

Below. Making a quill pen. (fig. 2)
Cut shaft of quill feather diagonally, trim off the end, then split nib up the centre to form the ink channel.

The quill pen was the drawing and writing tool used in the West until metal pens were introduced in the last century. It is a very responsive, flexible drawing instrument. If you can get hold of some goose, turkey or similar feathers, a quill pen is easy to make (try the butcher, perhaps, as a source). You'll need a very sharp, thin-bladed craft knife. Slice diagonally through the shaft of the feather near the tip, making a cut about 2cm (1in) long. Then split the centre of the nib approximately 6mm ($\frac{1}{4}$in) up. Finally sharpen the point down to whatever width you desire. Fig. 2 shows how to make a quill pen.

The reed pen is a traditional Oriental drawing instrument made from bamboo. This is a more rigid pen than the quill. It too is simple to make from a short length of bamboo that's about 1cm ($\frac{1}{2}$in) in diameter. Cut it in the same way as the feather, at a slope, and slit the centre. If there is any pithy stuff inside the bamboo, remove it.

Both the quill and reed are superb for rapid drawing. Any type of ink may be used with them.

Ballpoint pens can be used for drawing but, compared with the pens already mentioned, they are somewhat limited, insensitive tools. They have the advantage of not requiring the accompanying bottle of ink. Ballpoints are supplied with fine and medium points in a number of colours. The inks are inclined to fade.

Drawing with a pen on a vertical board is not a good idea. The ink runs back: at best inside the body of the pen, at worst, down your arm. Work seated or standing, with board or sketchbook at a slight slope.

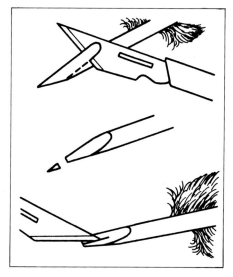

Fixative

Charcoal, pastel and chalk are pigments not contained in a gum or *vehicle*. Because they tend to smudge and eventually disappear such drawings should be fixed. Fixative is a resin and spirit mixture which is sprayed on to the drawing, giving it an invisible, non-shiny coating which secures the drawing to the paper. It is sold in aerosol cans or in bottles—to be applied with a spray diffuser. This is a little device of two hinged metal tubes. You place one end in the liquid and the other in your mouth, and blow. A fine mist spray comes out. Experiment on a scrap charcoal scribble first to see how far away you should be in order to avoid the spray making the drawing run. You'll also discover how hard you should blow. Wash and dry the diffuser after use or it may become blocked up.

You may use the fixative halfway through doing a drawing. Just wait a few seconds for it to dry before continuing.

Fixative should be used on all drawings executed in soft media which are liable to smudge; that is, drawings in very soft pencil, pastel or certain types of crayon.

Brushes

Drawing with a brush is a true pleasure. Because of the structure, natural hair brushes hold liquid better than those made with synthetic fibres. Buy a round sable hair watercolour brush for line and smaller scale washes, in say, size 4. These are expensive but infinitely preferable to the other types and, with due care, will last a long time. Sable hair is firm and springy and, as with all sympathetic tools, can be used to make the finest, delicate line or a bold dash. In comparison, line drawing with a squirrel hair brush is a sad, frustrating experience.

The squirrel, ox or blended hair brushes are best for use on a bigger scale for doing large areas of wash.

Polyester brushes are a reasonable alternative to sable. They are springy and will retain a fine point.

For broader brush drawing you may be interested in trying oil painting hogs' bristle brushes. These are shaped either oval, round, flat (like miniature house decorating brushes), or filbert—a cross between round and flat.

Nylon brushes, although very hardwearing, are not very suitable for wash drawing as they do not retain water well enough. They hold a paste-consistency medium better. They are totally unsuitable for fine line work.

All types of brushes are supplied in different qualities and, consequently, different prices. With the sable particularly, it's well worth buying one of the more expensive, fine quality brushes.

Always clean your brushes properly after use. Use cold water to remove ink and watercolour paints and white spirit to remove any oil-bound medium. To clean a brush thoroughly, after the initial rinsing, rub the bristles gently on a bar of soap and then in the palm of your hand

From left to right the brush shapes are oval, round, flat and filbert.

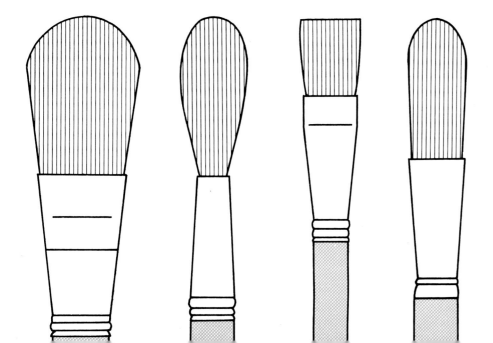

to create a lather. Rinse the brush under cold running water. Repeat this until the lather is clean. Finally rinse the brush thoroughly and shake the water from the bristles and shape it to a point in your lips.

Store your brushes standing vertically, bristles uppermost, in a jar. Don't lie them flat and certainly never stand them on their bristles.

Paints

Watercolour paint may be used as a drawing medium with a brush, either as a wash added to a line done in another material, or for making both washes and lines.

Oil paint too, diluted with turpentine, is used by a number of artists for direct, spontaneous drawing.

Craft knives

An essential adjunct to drawing is a knife. The kind of craft knife with easily replaceable blades made in different shapes is a useful tool. This means that the different blades will do for diverse jobs. You can keep certain of them sharp for cutting cardboard and paper, using the blunter blades for things like pencil sharpening.

Craft knives are sold by art supply shops and ironmongers or hardware stores. There are some inexpensive but effective types with plastic handles, and some all-metal types which are more expensive.

Drawing boards

You will need a rigid board on which to fix your drawing paper. An A1 size (841mm × 594mm [roughly 33in × 23in]) board is recommended as paper is being increasingly supplied in the international sizes. Drawing boards are available in different grades, so obviously are at different prices. If you treat it carefully (don't, for example, keep it leaning up against a hot radiator), an inexpensive board should last well. A smaller board in plywood or hardwood, measuring say, about 35cm x 25cm (14in x 10in), will be convenient to carry around and useful for drawing outdoors.

Don't use drawing-pins, thumb tacks or straight pins on your board. The holes they will make will obviously destroy the smooth surface and, after some years' use, lots of holes in the same area can actually break off the corners of the board. Attach your paper instead with bulldog clips, available at most stationers, or with drawing board clips, bought from an art shop. These will not damage the board or the paper.

Easels and the drawing position

An easel is not essential for drawing and it is certainly not a piece of equipment you need to buy at the beginning. The advantages of a good sturdy easel (not a cheap, wobbly one that falls over and comes unscrewed) are that it will hold your work vertically or at any angle you wish and at any height, so that you may stand or sit to draw. The box type of easel is very useful. It can be used indoors and out, and the box design means it will conveniently store and transport your materials too.

However, you may have no easel and yet wish to draw standing up, especially if you like working on a large scale. You can either fasten your paper to a suitable wall or to a large board which is then propped up against some furniture.

When you sit down to draw don't crouch over your work with the board horizontal in front of you; this is inclined to make your back ache. On a biggish drawing it means the far end is quite a long way away from you and a certain amount of visual distortion takes place; it also means that while you're drawing up at the far end, your drawing arm, and possibly part of your body, is covering an area of the drawing.

If you are seated at a table, prop your drawing board up against a pile of heavy books or something similar. There are table easels on the market with an adjustable slope.

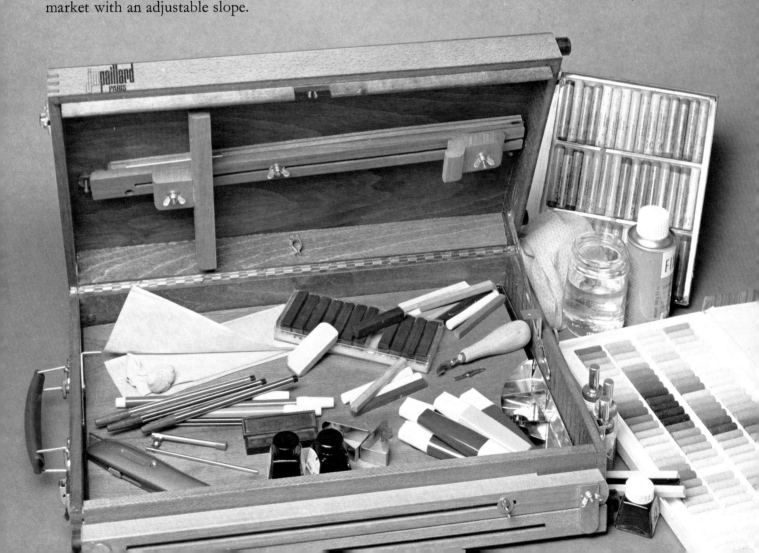

Frequently the reason you do not want to sit at a table is because the table will obstruct your view. So place another chair in front of you, with its back toward you, and lean your drawing board against the chair back.

When you are drawing a subject—a model or still life, say—endeavour to position yourself so that you need only to move your eyes and not your head or body between looking at the subject and looking at your work. The less intrusion between what you see and what you put down on paper the better.

Papers
Do experiment by trying out different media on some of the many kinds of papers available to see which combination you particularly like.

Paper is made in different weights, which means different thicknesses. Measurements vary but the large sheets, which is how you will normally buy paper, will measure Imperial [Standard] (775mm x 572mm) or Al (841mm x 594mm) [roughly 30½in x 22½in and 33in x 23in respectively].

Cartridge paper is relatively inexpensive and is the most widely used drawing paper. This is made in several different qualities and weights, and is always either white or cream. The surface will be found to vary in the different qualities and brands, some being very smooth, others fairly rough and textured. A good quality cartridge paper will suit all media.

Watercolour paper is a superior quality paper. The finest is still handmade but it is expensive. Mould-made papers use the same basic

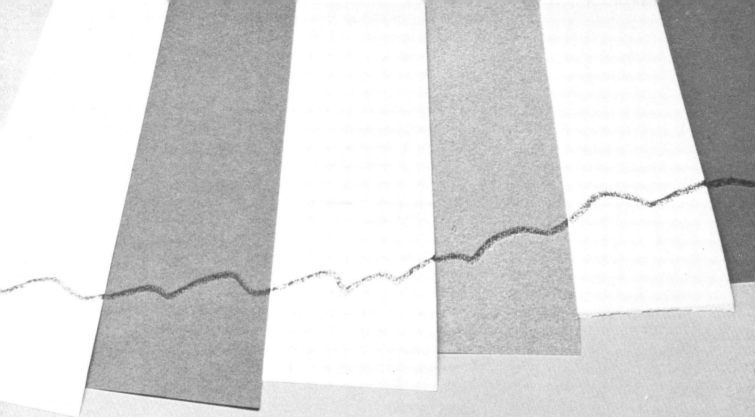

materials as handmade paper but they are made on a machine. Water-colour papers are white, off-white or cream. There are three types of finish: hotpressed or H.P., which is smooth; Rough, a coarsely textured surface; and Not, which is an intermediate, between heavily textured and smooth. The best quality watercolour papers are made from cotton rags, the less expensive from wood pulp. Although named 'watercolour paper', don't let this restrict its use; try pen, pencil, charcoal, etc. on it. The character is unique, and the paper will stand up to a great deal.

Ingres paper, made in white and a range of very attractive colours, has a slightly textured surface. Its distinctive feature is the hair-like pattern of fibres that runs all over it, so that a sheet will contain several colours, like a very fine tweed. Ingres paper is suitable for pastels, charcoal, Conté and ink work.

Sugar paper [construction paper] is a soft paper available in off-white and some muted colours. It is unsuitable for pencil and pen, but fine for pastels and similar media. It tends to fade.

Pastel paper, as the name implies, is primarily intended for pastel drawing. It is a better quality coloured paper than sugar paper. A good pastel paper has a *tooth*, that is, the type of texture that will hold the grains of pastel as it is drawn across the surface. Some of these papers, too, unfortunately fade.

Very cheap paper like newsprint (newspaper before it is printed) and lining [shelf lining] paper should be avoided for drawing. They do not respond well, tear easily and turn yellow after a short while. In prefer-ence, if you have no drawing paper handy, use writing or typing paper.

Detail paper is a very thin white paper, rather like the bank paper used for typing. Sometimes it is useful for tracing work. It is sold in pads, known as layout pads, or by the roll.

Tracing paper is available in sheet, roll or pad form.

Sketchbooks and pads

You can make up a sketchbook with your own selection of different types of paper in a loose-leaf binder or clipped to a small drawing board. Slip a large elastic band around the lower part to keep the sheets flat when not in use. When drawing outdoors the elastic band is often helpful if there is a breeze that would cause the sheets to be blown about.

Sketchbooks are on sale in a range of sizes. They have different types of binding: some are hard-backed and the stiff board cover folds right back, some are spiral bound and some have the pages pasted together along the top edge to form a pad. Sketchbooks are manufactured in cartridge, watercolour, pastel and Ingres papers. A sketch block has the pages pasted on all sides. You tear a sheet right off when you have finished with it.

The surface upon which you are working, that is, the support beneath your drawing paper, will affect the way in which your drawing instrument responds. Some, such as coloured pencils, work best on a hard, glossy underlay. So fix a sheet of hard, glossy cardboard or paper underneath your drawing paper. In other instances a softer support may prove more responsive—several sheets of newsprint, perhaps. Finding this out is very much a matter of experience and personal preference but it is certainly worth experimenting with different combinations. When drawing in your sketchbook it is helpful to slip a piece of cardboard

Paper should be stretched as shown here, if you intend to use a very wet drawing technique.

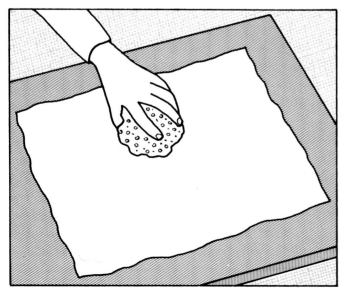
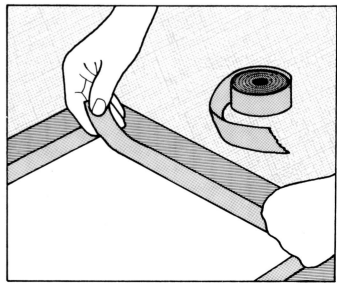

under the page you are using, both for the reasons just mentioned and also because it will protect the following pages.

Stretching paper

If you intend to use a very wet technique, a lot of fluid washes, for instance, it is advisable to stretch your paper first. This prevents it from buckling. Thoroughly dampen the paper with cold water and lay it out flat on the drawing board. Leave it for a minute or two to expand. Cut some brown paper gumstrip (not masking tape) to size for each edge. Dampen the gumstrip and, overlapping it about 1cm ($\frac{1}{2}$in) on the paper, stick the sheet of paper down onto the board. Place it flat so that the paper dries evenly. As it dries out, the paper will shrink slightly, resulting in a taut, flat surface. It will remain so when the wash is applied.

When the drawing is finished and quite dry remove the paper by pulling the gumstrip away; any left adhering to the drawing can be trimmed off; any on the drawing board may be removed by dampening.

Scraperboard

In most types of drawing, dark lines are made on a light background. With black scraperboard the reverse applies. The board is a sheet of cardboard coated first with a specially prepared white chalk and then with a layer of black ink. The drawing is made by scratching through the black ink. This gives a very precise white mark. Drawing can be done with special scraperboard tools, which are like pen nibs and fit into an ordinary pen holder, or any kind of scratching implement. The blade of a craft knife is particularly versatile. Use it without the handle as this means you can slope it at all sorts of angles. To make it more comfortable

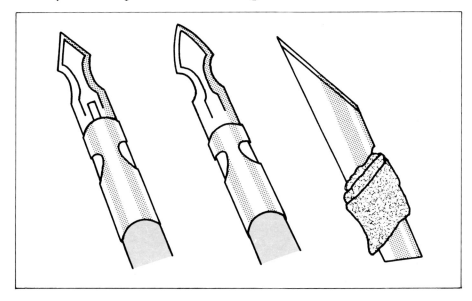

The tools at the left and middle are specially made for use on scraperboard, the one on the right is a home-made tool made by binding a scalpel blade to a pen holder.

and safer to hold, bind a little adhesive tape around the end you are holding.

There is also a white scraperboard available. You can draw on it in black Indian ink with a pen or brush and then (after ascertaining that the ink is completely dry) use the scratching technique too. Try out coloured scraperboards as well. Use watercolour or ink to coat the prepared white board. Make some tests first, though, because some colours penetrate the chalk coating. This means the scratches won't show up as white lines.

Avoid bending your scraperboard as this cracks the coating. For this reason, always cut it with a craft knife against a metal ruler, not with scissors.

Dandelions, *Joseph Harrison*.
A scraperboard can be used for highly detailed white on black drawing.

A Handling Colour

The mixing of colour has its own simple basic rules, so once you have learned them you will know how to control your palette. Paints are used in this chapter for the examples but the same principles apply to coloured inks, pastels, crayons and so on. For colour experiments use a good, opaque white ground (the surface on which you paint; sized or oil painting paper is best). Any colour, cream, for example, would influence the colours.

The three *primary* colours are red, yellow and blue. They are called primary because they cannot be mixed from other colours, that is, you can't make red, yellow and blue. In theory you should be able to mix all the colours you wish with different proportions of red, yellow and blue. They represent all the colours there are. In practice, this doesn't work because it is impossible to manufacture pigments that do not contain traces of other colours. Again, in theory, if you mix all three primaries together you should get black but, for the reasons already mentioned, you would end up with a darkish grey. But the principle is the same— mix all the three primaries together and you get a 'non-colour'.

Battle *by Kandinsky.*
This artist explored the use of colour as a means of expressing emotion.

It is virtually impossible to find a true red, a true yellow and a true blue because of the fact that all colours tend to have traces of other colours in them. A compromise, which partially gets around this problem, and at the same time gives you an excellent range of colours for mixing and general use, is to choose two versions of each primary colour. Here is a recommended basic set of colours, accompanied by the reasons for choosing them. The names correspond with the Winsor and Newton colour chart for Artist's Oil Colours. These particular names may not be used for these particular colours in another medium—pastels, for instance, or in another brand, but you can compare the colours visually with the chart.

Cadmium yellow—is a yellow containing some of the primary colour red.

Cadmium lemon yellow—contains traces of the primary colour blue.

Cadmium red—is a red veering slightly towards the primary colour yellow.

Alizarin crimson—is a red which contains some blue.

Cobalt blue—has a little yellow in it.

French Ultramarine blue—contains a little red.

Ivory black—blacks can be brownish, greenish or bluish; aim for as neutral a black as possible and one that is good and dense.

Titanium white—not a transparent, silvery or bluish white.

Unfortunately the names of colours are not standardized, so what may be called magenta in one manufacturer's paint or ink is a totally different colour when made by another company.

Because the mixing theory does not actually work in practice—you cannot achieve a clear, brilliant purple by mixing—Winsor violet is recommended. Similarly, you may like to purchase Viridian green too. The colour wheel is a traditional way of showing how colours relate to one another. This is how to make your own version of the colour wheel. It will teach you a great deal about the mixing of colours. Keep it, it will be very useful to refer to later.

Have ready a pure white ground. Use each of the colours straight from the tube. Be particular about the brushes being clean, so that the colours remain pure and untainted. First, paint an area of the Cadmium yellow and next to it a similar sized area of Cadmium lemon. On the Cadmium lemon side, working around in a circle, add Cobalt (the blue that contains yellow), next, French Ultramarine. Then paint the Alizarin crimson area. This follows on as it is the red containing some blue. Finally paint in the Cadmium red section.

On the palette try mixing the primary colours together until you have achieved a neutral grey that doesn't lean in the direction of any of its three components. You cannot do this by combining precisely measured equal amounts of each colour. Some colours are inherently darker or stronger than others so you must judge the quantities by carefully watching the mixtures. Try the mixed colours out on scrap paper. When you have achieved as neutral a colour as you can, paint a patch of it in the centre of the triangle formed by the three patches of red, yellow and blue.

Secondary colours are pure (not 'greyed') colours mixed from any pair of primary colours. They are orange, green and purple. Mix the Cadmium yellow and Cadmium red to get a clear orange, visually mid-way between yellow and red. Paint a rough arc around the outside of the yellow and red patches. Make a green from the Cadmium lemon and Cobalt and paint a green arc around the yellow and blue section. The purple, as previously mentioned, is difficult to make. However, for this experiment, mix the best purple you can from the Alizarin and Ultramarine and complete the outer circle by painting in the purple arc.

Each of the three secondary colours is a mixture of two of the primary colours. For instance, purple is made of red and blue. The remaining primary colour is yellow and yellow is the *complementary* colour of

This is how the finished colour wheel should appear.

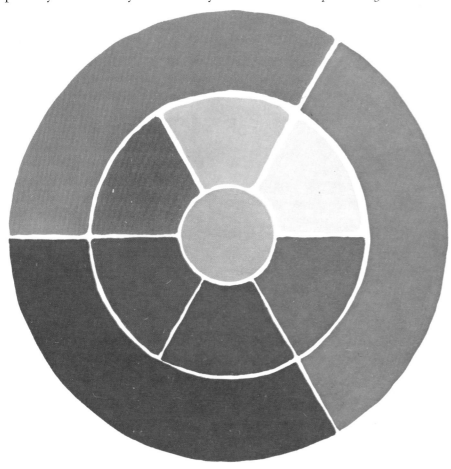

purple. Any pair of complementary colours when mixed together will tend to go grey or 'non-coloured' because you are again combining the three primaries—mixing together all the colours there are. From your own painted colour circle you can see which colours form complementary pairs. Look at a primary colour patch. The arc of colour opposite it on the far side of the circle is its complementary colour, i.e. the colour which is made by combining the remaining two primaries.

Try some experimental mixing, working gradually from one colour, Cadmium yellow for example, adding increasingly larger amounts of purple (yellow's complementary colour). Paint small patches of the mixed colours on paper to keep a record of the strange 'mid-way' colours you will achieve. Adding a touch of the colour's complement will always dull it down—but not in the dreary way that splodging black into it does. Yellow is extremely light in tone, purple is quite dark. Purple is a very powerful colour, and, as you add it to the yellow, be very sparing. A small amount of purple will have a dramatic effect upon the yellow. Follow this by mixing other pairs of complementary colours.

The type of mixing used so far in these colour experiments has all

been done on the palette, prior to applying the paint to the ground. This is the method most generally adopted when using oil paints. However, oil paint is extremely versatile and can also be used in the ways suggested for the other types of media.

Colour mixtures with drawing materials like coloured pencils or crayons, felt pens or pastels can be produced by laying down one colour in a series of strokes and then laying another colour over it, and so on. Here you can vary the closeness of the strokes and, depending upon how hard you press, the strength of the colour. There are infinite variations. The first base colour, a light blue, for example, may be solid with no white paper showing through. The second colour, red, might be applied in an open cross-hatching. At this point you will have produced a slightly irregular-looking purple. Add some dots of yellow and some dashes of green. The effect is very like a woollen tweed. Tweed is, in fact, made up in a very similar way from little dots or lines of different colours. The colours mix optically—that is, as you look at them they appear to merge together. Heather mixture, a type of tweed, is just like its name, all different colours—imagine the colours in a real heath.

Modern half-tone reproduction uses a system of red, yellow, blue and black dots to print a photograph. Thus the primaries are used to create the colours and the black to provide tone.

When you are next standing by a large advertisement with a photographic image on it, try to take a really close look at the surface to see how it is made up. The sun-tanned thigh of the lady on the beach will be seen to be a myriad of different coloured dots. Half tone colour printing breaks a coloured phtograph down into these dots. All the red dots are printed from a red printing plate, the blue dots from a blue plate, and so on. The whole combines optically to read as a normal, full-coloured image. Georges Seurat, the Frenchman who lived from 1859 to 1891, was an artist who exploited the idea of visual or optical mixing to the full. He followed the ideas about colour that Delacroix, and then the Impressionists, introduced. They were moving away from the rigid attitudes of Neo-Classical art which prevailed in the late-eighteenth and early-nineteenth centuries. They studied, drew and painted from real living subject matter, observing the effect of light upon the appearance of things. Seurat's technique is known as pointillism (although he himself preferred to call it divisionism). He used small dots of primary and secondary colours, intermingled to read, in the same way as the printed poster, as figures, scenes, etc. He was a master of design and a superb draughtsman. In the hands of a lesser artist such a scientific approach could have deteriorated into a boring, mechanical exercise.

Try out the optical mixing methods with your own materials. Try different proportions of both the colours themselves and the white paper, mixing them together. A strong, sturdy paper may be required if, as with felt pens, the surface tends to roughen up. The manner in which you apply the colours can, at the same time as creating new optically mixed colours, suggest textural qualities too. Circular scribbling marks, for instance, might combine with cross-hatching.

Laying a wash of one colour over another is an alternative colour mixing technique. This lends itself particularly to watercolour and coloured ink work as these are transparent media. One colour will show through another. You can combine washes of different strengths and solid washes with broken ones (i.e. incomplete areas with the gaps allowing the other colour to show through unevenly).

Experiment with a technique that is a combination of the two above methods. Water soluble coloured pencils are particularly suited to this. Lay down a wash of colour and, while it's still wet, draw in dots, dashes or spots of another colour on top of it. These will partly merge into the background colour but will still retain a slightly uneven quality.

Each colour you use—each tube of paint, each crayon—is comprised of these elements: hue, tone, brilliance, warmth or coldness, opacity or transparency and associated qualities. Therefore, each colour, like each person, has its own character and traits. To further the comparison, each behaves in a particular way in a given situation. None is ever seen alone, without interrelating, being affected by and affecting the others.

La Poudreuse, *an oil painting by Georges Seurat who helped to develop the method of optical mixing by using dots of pure colour side by side on the canvas. This style is sometimes called pointillism.*

The above terms, hue, tone and so on, are unfortunately interpreted in different ways and diverse words are used to mean, in effect, the same thing. In this book the definitions are as follows. *Hue*—the actual colour itself, green as distinct from red. *Tone*—how light or dark a colour appears. Imagine looking at a still life group of objects which are, as always in normal conditions, many-coloured. Try to think how light or dark the various colours are in relation to one another. Is the apple darker than the orange? It is rather as if you were seeing the objects as a black and white photograph, replacing the colours by an equivalent range of greys, running through from black to white. *Brilliance*—how much a colour glows or shows up. Brilliance is especially influenced by

Sonia Delaunay Terk 1913

the surrounding colours. *Warmth or coldness*—some colours actually appear to come toward you and these are called warm colours; others seem to recede and are known as cool colours. *Opacity or transparency*—these two aspects very much relate to the medium you are using. Within one medium (oil paints, for example) the covering ability (opacity) or lack of it (transparency) can vary greatly from one colour to another. *Associated qualities*—colour is a very emotive subject, perhaps still forming a powerful link with our ancient past. We still have strong associated ideas about what colours are 'correct' for what purposes. Who, for instance, would fancy eating a plateful of blue cauliflower?

Local Colour is the term used for the inherent colour of an article. The local colour of a ripe tomato is red, although on close inspection the fruit may prove to look white or pale blue in the highlight areas and may be purple or brown in the shadows. *Reflected colour* is, as the name implies, colour reflected from one object to another. Place a white cup next to the tomato and the outside of the cup near the tomato will pick up a pinkish glow. The nature and texture of a surface very much affects the way in which it reflects light and thus colour, and is also influenced by other colours. Caucasian flesh is very susceptible to colour reflection. Recall the 'Do you like butter' game played by children. The child holds a buttercup under a person's chin. If the chin looks yellow, as in good clear lighting conditions it almost certainly will because of reflecting the yellow flower, the person does like butter.

Additional terms to define are: a *shade*, which is a colour with black added to it: a *tint*, a colour with white added to it. Strictly speaking, 'pastel shade' is a distinct contradiction in terms. In certain media, watercolour or coloured inks, for example, tints are obtained not by adding white, which would make the colour mixture more opaque, but by adding water, thereby allowing more of the white paper background to shine through the colour to lighten it. Similarly, with crayons and coloured pencils a lighter application of the colour will produce a tint version of that colour.

In order to really begin to acquaint yourself with the fascinations of colour, colour mixing and matching, try doing some colour studies. Choose a theme, say, green, and gather together several different green items. Choose things of a small scale for this project. These could be a leaf, a length of ribbon and a ball of knitting wool, all laid on a sheet of green paper. Immediately, the diversity within the term 'green' will become glaringly apparent. Create a composition, a coloured painting or coloured drawing, with the specific aim of matching up the colours in the little still life group.

Try to fix which object, or which part of an object (and this is going to be difficult), is a real, true green. That means a green that is not bluish or brownish or yellowish, and at the same time is mid-toned and not too

Left. Etude de Lumière: Prismes Electriques, *Sonia Delaunay. A mixture of drawing mediums— watercolour and pastel—used to create colour mixes. Notice how secondary colours are formed where the primary colours intermingle.*

Right. Le Bain, *Suzanne Valadon, pastel. The warmth of the ground colour and the use of warm shades of normally cool colours helps to convey a feeling of intimacy in this scene.*

Far right. Strand Hotel, Rangoon, 1971, *David Hockney, pencil. The brilliance of the primary colours enhances the feeling of airy space in a bright hotel lobby.*

dark or too pale. The local colour of an object, as you will see here, is greatly altered and influenced by its surroundings, so you may find you have to select one tiny part of an object as your 'true' green patch. Use this true green as your guide. Compare other greens in the group— is this part of the leaf like the true green? If not, why not? Is it different in actual hue? Is it somehow a duller green (perhaps it contains some red, its complement) or is it a much darker toned colour all together? How does it compare in tone with the rest of the articles in the arrangement, including the green paper background?

Field of Corn in the Moonlight,
Samuel Palmer, ink and watercolour.
Colour conveys mood, and in this
night-time landscape the use of
purple warmed by red gives the
viewer a comfortable feeling of
tranquillity.

While observing the colours don't, of course, forget about the shapes, proportions, and so on of the over-all composition. After you have completed your green study move the objects onto a white paper background and arrange them in the same way as before. See how now the colours and the general appearance of the items seem so different. Each object shows up as much more clearly defined. Its outside shape can be seen much better because of the contrast between the green lines and the white background, and also because of the strength of tone of the greens against the white. Also, the non-colour background makes it easier to discern the strength of the various greens.

If possible try to take your little green and white still life into some entirely different kind of lighting conditions to see what a marked effect light has upon colour. We come upon this all the time in our everyday life. You take a bolt of fabric to the door of the shop to see what colour it really is, knowing that artificial lighting can't be trusted. An example of this is trying to find a pale-coloured car in a sodium-lit car park. In those lighting conditions, all the light-coloured cars look a similar sort of yellow ochre colour.

This light and colour phenomenon is deeply ingrained in our lives. There are many commonly used phrases associated with it which conjure up moods: the blues, blue with cold; black depression; in the pink; to see red; to ginger up. The warm/cool idea is not only a visually apparent occurence, it is linked up with associated ideas in language too. The blue associations are cold and dull; the red connections are warm and fiery.

To see further effects of colour against colour, still using the green objects, slide some different coloured paper backgrounds under them. The complementary colour of green is, as you know, red. It is the colour most unlike green, most opposite to green. Place a piece of a middle (Cadmium) red paper under your most true green item. As the background colour is now the most opposite to the colour of the object, the object will appear at its most intensely green. The maximum brilliance of the green is now being displayed.

This method of using complementary colours to enhance each other's brilliance was a favourite device of the Op artists of the 1960s. By placing complementary colours that are the same tone side by side, the edge where they meet will begin to dance as the colours move back and forth optically. This occurs because the colours are the same tone and one does not dominate the other.

The gummed coloured paper squares that are sold in packets intended for craft work are very useful for these kinds of colour experiment projects. The colours are flat and clear. Buy a packet and try different colour combinations. Another interesting facet of colour can be seen by varying the proportions of the area of one colour to another. This can be used to alter the importance of a colour.

Having considered these ideas, look out particularly for these instances in whatever subject matter you are going to examine for your drawings.

Colour is an immensely emotive and strangely irrational subject. People will say that they have a certain favourite colour, for reasons they can't define, or that they never wear green because it is unlucky. Associated qualities play an extraordinarily strong part. The following experiment produced some very interesting results. A group of art students were asked to paint small, 5 cm (2 in) squares of different colours. These were then to be arranged together into groups—groups

Watercolour study of a bird's wing by Albrecht Dürer. A close observation of colour as it appears in nature will reveal that even the subtlest colour is a blend of many.

of squares of colours that they really like together, and groups of squares of colours that they detested together. The colour samples were to be flatly painted in oil paints and accurately cut out into identically sized squares. Any type of colour mixing was permissible. Oil paints were used because (as with the examples at the beginning of this chapter) there is the greatest range of colours. The flat, non-textured painted square shape was chosen to remove, as far as possible, any associations that could be linked with the shape itself or the surface quality. The students dutifully set about preparing their little squares with the accompanying mutterings of: 'What a hideous pink', and 'I can't stand purple', etc. The final outcome of the project, when the sets of colours were displayed on the wall, produced the surprising fact that nobody, in spite of their earlier protestations, could honestly find a pair, let alone a group of colours, that they disliked. As anonymous patches of colour, not being applied to anything, they were all acceptable. Immediately when uses for the colours were suggested, the likes and dislikes arose—quite vehemently. A pair consisting of a sage green and a greyish-brownish beige (how impossible it is to describe colours verbally), when considered rendered in glossy paint as a bathroom decoration scheme, produced howls of dismay. Yet the same green and beige pair would make an elegant and highly sophisticated watered silk evening dress. It is only when seen in context, not as abstract concepts, that colours appear appropriate or otherwise.

Project: A Self Portrait

Drawing a human figure as your initial attempt may possibly seem a daunting prospect. Your response may be: 'But I can't even draw an apple!' Consider the following reasons for doing a self-portrait.

Virtually everyone would like to draw people and faces. A human being is, of course, a complicated object—or *subject,* as the thing you are drawing is usually called. But you are particularly familiar with the appearance of this specific human being, having studied it in the mirror every day for many years. You know the way its hair falls, the very texture of that hair, the way it won't go in a certain direction; you have first-hand knowledge of the structure of the face—the roundness or gauntness of it, the lumps and bumps on this particular nose—and so on. If you draw yourself, you, the model, will be available whenever it suits you, the artist, to work. You may find, once you get under way, that you'll wish to return to, and work on, the drawing at odd times.

If you ask a friend to model for your first drawing there is inevitably going to be a slightly awkward situation. Your sitter is bound to want to see the drawing. You may feel that politeness requires you to flatter—rather than the reverse, which may well occur. As you struggle with your drawing, which probably doesn't look like much at all during certain stages of its development, you can well do without uninformed criticism or advice. Doing a self-portrait is beautifully private. For your first, quite possibly fumbling attempts, you will be alone, thereby avoiding any sort of embarrassment. You've no need to be constantly conscious of your model's well-being—is he or she comfortable, getting bored, cold, thirsty, etc? You can wrestle with your problems, get in a mess, plod on and endeavour to sort things out, becoming fully involved and free of interference. So, have a try. This is how you set things up.

Choose a place to do your drawing where you won't be disturbed and where you won't be disturbing others. You want to avoid being pressured by anything. Doing a drawing means you need time to think. You are going to be studying the subject, making the marks and judging and weighing up all the various factors. Not an easy thing to do without complete solitude, and virtually impossible with the baby crawling all over you or the television going at full blast. So, if you can, work in

Self portrait by Edward Munch, charcoal and chalk on canvas.

41

With the light source below, an attractive face takes on a sinister cast. So light not only influences the appearance of objects and surroundings, but how we react to them.

seclusion, preferably in a room where you can leave your drawing things set up; or where they can easily be stored, unpacked and re-assembled whenever you wish to continue.

Try to think of this self-portrait as something that is going to take a considerable amount of time. There's no need to do it all in one go, unless you have the time available and wish to do so. There's no need to limit yourself to one drawing only. All creative processes spark off ideas and you may wish to explore and develop such thoughts in other drawings. Keep several going at the same time if you wish.

Returning to continue work on an unfinished drawing often has the advantage that, during the time you've been away from it, further thoughts have formed (possibly subconsciously) about how you might tackle certain areas. Also, a fresh new look may make you realize that you had become too involved in one section or one aspect, to the detriment of the rest of the composition.

Arrange your paper and drawing board as described previously, and have ready all your materials and some scrap paper on which to try things out. Fix up a mirror so that you can look with ease, moving your eyes only, from mirror to drawing and *vice versa*. Do make sure that both the mirror and the drawing board are properly supported and that neither is likely to crash to the floor in the middle of the proceedings.

The height, the distance from you, and the angle at which you place the looking glass will affect the view you see of yourself framed within the mirror. Experiment with these three factors, height, distance and angle and observe how the apparent size of your face and body alters in relation to the area of the room you can see as you move the mirror about.

The way in which light falls upon an object influences its appearance and consequently our response to its appearance. This is happening all the time, wherever we are, in many, many subtle ways. We are familiar with certain well-known instances. The older woman, when dining out, blesses the candles that are so much kinder to her wrinkles and grey hairs than a 150 watt electric bulb would be! Brilliant sunshine will transform a beach which yesterday, under the clouds, looked like the end of the world. A face lit from below can appear quite fearsome (a popular device in the making of horror films) but the same face with a more usual top or side lighting becomes benevolent. So, consider the lighting for your self-portrait. Is it going to remain constant, an electric light in the same position, for instance? Or will the changing time of day alter the look of things? If so, and you intend to work on the drawing at different times of the day, it may be wise to take some simple precautions before you begin. As artificial light is unchanging, possibly you should work under electric light, with the curtains drawn too—if the light coming through the window has a strong influence on what you see.

This may all seem like a lot of fuss, but if you remove as far as is possible, any extraneous disturbances that are likely to occur you will be able to work with much more concentration. You'll also be confident that, when you return to continue your drawing, possibly a day or so later, things will still look the same.

Decide upon which view of yourself in the looking glass you want to draw. Don't choose some fantastically awkward pose or a position that is going to be very difficult to resume after each time you move. Relax. Don't attempt to draw yourself smiling, frowning or clenching a pipe between your teeth—you'll never be able to sustain the pose.

Here are just a few suggestions to get you started. Roughly draw in the main shape of your head (and, if you're drawing the body or part of it, that too) to make sure you will be able to get all you want onto the paper. You might think too, of using the edge of the mirror as a sort of frame around your drawing, actually drawing it in. This kind of device can prove a great aid to sorting out the relative positions of things in a drawing. For instance, does your left ear come halfway down the edge of the mirror—that kind of thing.

Think how one part of anything is built up upon another part. In the case of your head, there's a firm underlying base—the skull. Use your sense of·touch to help you work out how the vertical egg shape of the face part swells out into the spherical shape at the back of the skull. Feel how your neck, which is a cylinder, supports and pushes up into the egg shape and the sphere. Study the way your face is divided into planes, or

Fig. 1 Self portrait by Leonardo da Vinci, red chalk.

43

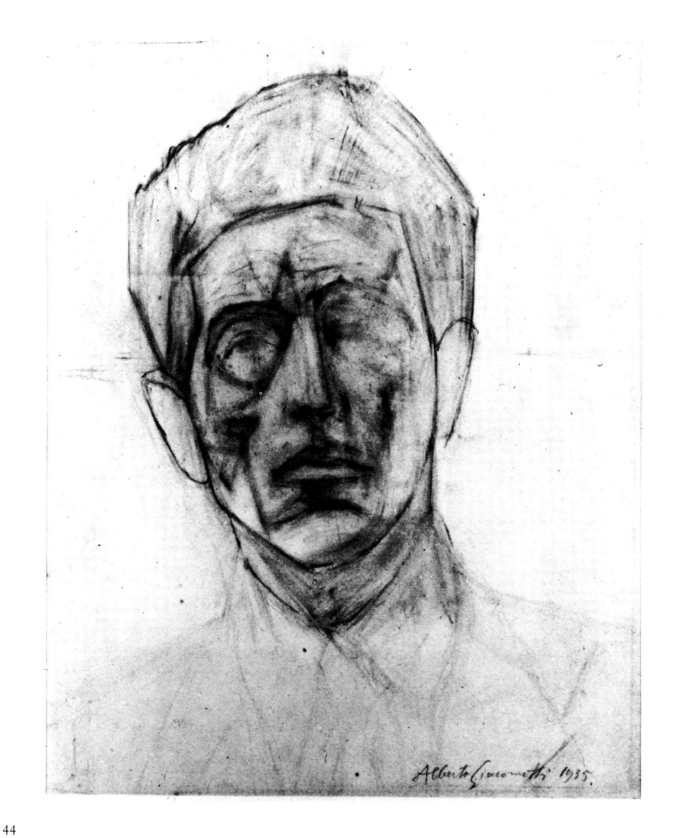

surfaces, sloping in different directions, running gradually or sharply from one to another. Look at the way the nose is a collection of planes sticking out from a flatter area. Think again of the skull. Even if you are not very familiar with its shape, you will recall that there are large, dark holes where the eyes go. In your living face, these holes, the eye sockets, are filled by the spherical eyeball, surrounded by all the muscles, fat and skin that make up the eyelids and so on in that section of your head. Thinking a little about how your face and head are constructed will help you to understand better what you are looking at.

Now, continuing all the time to look closely, work within your roughly drawn shape, gradually building up the portrait. If you realize the first drawn shape is wrong somewhere, alter it. Nothing is sacrosanct. Alter, change and improve anything you like.

Use whatever methods you wish to put across your thoughts. If drawing shadows seems like a good way of explaining how the head is solid and how the nose protrudes, use shadows. If you become fascinated

Fig. 2 (left) Self portrait by Alberto Giacometti, pencil.

Fig. 3 Self portrait by Janet Allen, pencil.

by the apparent edges of things and a fine line would seem appropriate—use a fine line.

Consider, and think how to express in drawing terms, the way the skin or the flesh of the lips is so different from that of the cheek. How do you convey the quality of the hair? How do you make it seem to grow from the head?

Remember you are very fortunate. You have plenty of knowledge and inside information about this particular model.

The intention of a drawing is to convey ideas visually to the viewer. Describing a drawing verbally can be rather futile, but here it seems worth trying in order to start you thinking about and looking at other self-portraits to find aspects that you too have encountered in your own work.

Leonardo da Vinci's self-portrait (fig. 1) was drawn in red chalk when

H. Matisse 9/39

H. matisse 10/39

H matisse

H. matisse 10/39

47

he was about sixty years old. He is one of the greatest draughtsmen the world has ever known, and his supreme confidence and control of the medium are well displayed here. The delicate line work instantly conveys the idea of thinning white hair; the subtle shading shows the slight slackness of older flesh.

The self-portrait by painter/sculpter Alberto Giacometti (fig. 2) was drawn in 1935. At that time the artist was working a great deal from the human head, sculpting and drawing. This pencil drawing is clearly very much concerned with solidity and the planes of the structure.

The self-portrait by Janet Allen in fig. 3 shows the face reflected in a multi-convex mirror. This produces a complex set of different reflections of the head and the background behind the head. This makes fascinating repeating, but slightly differing effects, especially with the patterned clothing. Pencils ranging from 6B to 4H were used on a rough textured watercolour paper.

Henri Matisse's self-portrait (fig. 4) is an etching, that is a print from a drawing made, in this case, directly from the subject straight onto the etching plate. The fine etched line is similar to the sort of line a very fine barrel pen will give. See how the different methods of *cross-hatching* (criss-crossing lines) build up tones of different strengths. Compare it to the four Matisse drawings, also self-portraits, in fig. 5, which were done thirty-five years later than this one. Those thirty-five years were packed with concentrated drawing, painting and sculpting.

A Elements of Composition

Now that you have had some practical experience of drawing you will appreciate the points to be discussed in this chapter. Reading endless theorizing without having tried any drawing could easily frighten you off.

Think about how you got on with your self-portrait. Does the composition of your drawing look right? That is to say, does the figure seem to be placed in a satisfactory way on the piece of paper, or does it appear to be slipping to one side or slithering downwards out of the bottom of the picture? Composition—the very word 'composed' has a dual meaning, 'constructed' and 'restful'—means sorted out and organized within the area of the paper on which you are drawing. This does not mean that the entire surface of the paper must be filled in with drawing. There is nothing wrong with doing so, but alternatively, there is nothing wrong with drawing the figure isolated, but composed within the paper space. Compare the Picasso portrait in Techniques with these two approaches in mind. However you go about your drawing, packing it

Look about you and notice how the surroundings often form natural compositions.

49

full or being highly economical with your lines, you must be selective about the arrangement, or the design, within the paper shape.

Composing and/or designing is an entirely natural function. Everyone appears to start life with an inherent sense of design. Just look at the way children will draw, selecting and deciding on arrangements and colours as they go along. We all do it, to a greater or lesser degree, every day. Each morning you comb and arrange your hair and choose what to wear with what. You have definite preferences for certain designs, styles and shapes in all things, but especially so in the subjects which particularly interest you, be they cars, gardening, cake decoration or postage stamps.

In most cases, because of the nature of our modern lives, this designing ability becomes very much pushed into the background, not to say atrophied. There's doubtless a small vestige still lurking there and, having taken up drawing, you can encourage it to grow.

When you take a photograph you automatically compose the picture. You look through the viewfinder and, if your aunt has no head, you move the camera around so that her head appears inside the picture shape. Then you probably will go a step further and, assuming her patience will hold out, you move the picture space around to accommodate other things, part of the rose bush, a little of the lawn or whatever. This is composing and designing.

When you decide to study something with a view to drawing it, a whole gamut of experiences hits the senses. In the open air, contemplating a scene, there are all the physical experiences of the weather conditions. Perhaps the sun is burning hot, making your drawing paper glare; maybe there's an irritating cold breeze which, because you are standing still will gradually numb you to the bone. There are all the sounds—bees buzzing, traffic noise, birds singing; all the smells; the sensation underfoot of coarse grass, ploughed field or tarmac; in short, complete awareness. One of the great delights of taking up drawing is that it necessitates your putting yourself into a calm, reflective frame of mind, in order to be ready to concentrate and observe.

Similarly, faced with a still life, you not only see the objects sitting there, past experience instantly feeds you with numerous facts and thoughts. You know the slight rubbery feel of an orange without actually touching it and you recall its delicious smell. You know that a drinking glass is hard and shiny and that the basket is of a totally different texture and would creak if you were to touch it.

When drawing a figure—your own or someone else's, it is impossible to look at that person solely as an object. Initially all your preconceived impressions are bound to come welling up.

So, with all this diverse knowledge flooding in, how do you sort out something to put down on your paper?

If a solid three-dimensional object is shown on a two-dimensional, or flat, surface a great deal of selection must take place during the translation process. A camera, which produces a two-dimensional image of an object, makes the selection by recording only the effect of light falling on the object; if there is insufficient light, the camera simply does not record the object.

A camera doesn't reproduce the 'touchable' qualities of the object, although a good photograph will evoke them.

The colour photograph of the still life shown here can be seen as one stage in the selecting process. It is of an arrangement of coloured shapes on paper. The black and white photograph overleaf is another stage of the selecting process—not inferior, merely different. In the coloured photograph the very fact that the colour is still there means that the image is in one way more representative of the actual objects. Not so much selection or discarding has taken place as in the black and white

Below. The still life group shown here illustrates the ability of colour to add a particular dimension to an image.

photograph. Here the colours have been changed into different degrees of grey, ranging through from black to white. The camera has had to decide whether to represent a green area, for instance, as black or a dark grey. In a similar way, when you are going to make a drawing, you must decide how you are going to represent the multi-coloured, three-dimensional objects before you on a flat, two-dimensional sheet of paper, using the kind of marks your particular drawing tool makes.

The statement, 'I wish I could draw' surely means, 'I wish I could put over visually what I feel about the thing I am looking at.' It seems, as with word communication, that there are twin aspects to learning to draw. First, there is the physical dexterity—in language this means either getting your tongue around the pronunciation or coping with handwriting, two things we generally master at a very early age. Secondly, comes the organization and expression of ideas—a vastly more complex affair.

Below. This is a black and white reproduction of the still life shown on the previous page. The printing process has translated the colours into different shades of grey.

Consider this parallel in relation to learning to draw. First, you must have some sort of control over the drawing instrument. This control will develop the more drawing you do.

Now think about the second similarity. As with composition in the language or literary sense, there is also a basic 'grammar' for the visual arts. In order to communicate an idea in words one person will compose a sentence according to certain principles which are understood by those with whom he is communicating. These principles are so well known that the speaker does not have to think about them at all. This only happens when he encounters a new medium, as for example, when he attempts to speak in a foreign language.

You are going to make drawing the vehicle for your ideas. So what are the basic principles of the grammar of drawing—the components that make up a composition?

To begin with you must plan your drawing. You want to be sure that you will be able to get all you want to onto your piece of paper. A helpful device is the viewfinder. This acts in the same way as the view-finder of a camera. It helps you to decide how much to incorporate out of what you see in front of you, isolating an area from its surroundings, thus enabling you to study that section in particular without being sidetracked.

Before making a viewfinder just try this simple experiment. Form your thumb and first finger to enclose a roughly square space. Hold your hand as far from your eye as you can and look at the view out of the window or within the room through the little square space. Move your hand around, still with your arm extended, so that you see different little pictures enclosed in the finger-thumb frame. Now bring your hand much closer to your eye. You will notice how much more of the view you can see when the frame is closer to your eye.

To make a simple viewfinder, cut out two L-shaped pieces of cardboard (cornflake boxes are fine for this). They should each measure 10cm (4in) along each inside edge. The width of the frame should be approximately 4cm ($1\frac{1}{2}$in). Having two L-shapes means you can combine them to make any sort of rectangular viewing space shape. Fig. 1 shows how to use a viewfinder.

Having decided on the shape of the rectangle you want, you can hold the frame together in that position with paper clips. They can then easily be unstuck and reassembled in a different shape for use with another drawing.

The viewfinder loses all its effectiveness if you set out to draw on a piece of paper which is not the same shape, i.e. a rectangle in the same proportion as the viewfinder itself. An easy way of ensuring that proportions relate is to lay the viewfinder on the paper so that two adjacent sides of the hole correspond with the top left-hand corner of

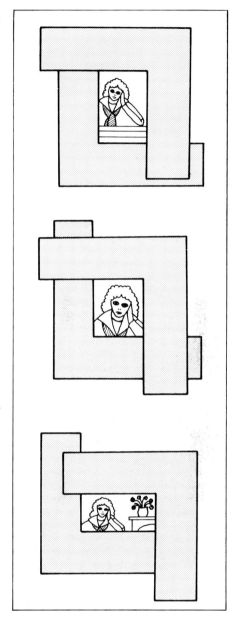

Fig. 1 A viewfinder will help you to decide which part of the scene to draw and how to arrange a successful composition.

53

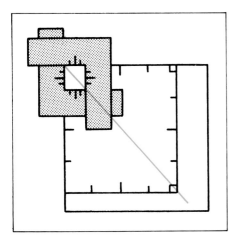

Use the viewfinder to establish an area of similar proportion on your drawing paper. (*Fig. 2*)

the paper. Lightly rule a diagonal line through the viewfinder rectangle and across your drawing paper. (It doesn't matter that the line will have a gap in it where it passes over the lower right-hand corner of the viewfinder frame.) Decide upon the size you want to draw within. Draw a line at a right angle to the top edge of the paper down to the diagonal line. At this point, where it meets the diagonal line, draw another line across, again at a right angle and parallel with the bottom edge of the paper, out to the left-hand edge. This forms a rectangle which is larger, but the same shape as, the viewfinder. Fig. 2 shows how to do this.

A further useful aid is to measure and divide the edges of the viewfinder hole into half and quarter measurements. Use a soft pencil which can be erased later. Lightly indicate on your drawing paper these half and quarter measurements too.

Each time you hold the viewfinder up you must be sure your hand is in the same position relative to your eye. Otherwise (as you saw in the thumb and forefinger experiment), the size of everything will be vastly altered. The half and quarter measurement markers will help you to establish the position of things: that tree in the landscape corresponds with the three-quarter mark; the roof shape fits vertically just left of the halfway mark and horizontally is just above the halfway mark. It means that, instead of being faced with a slightly frightening expanse of plain paper, you have some practical aids to help you get the drawing going.

As with all the grammar guidelines, the viewfinder procedure can be used with most kinds of subject matter. It will help you organize a still life or a drawing from the figure (it should steer you around that common pitfall of finding you can't get the feet in).

Regrettably, the viewfinder device does not work in such a straightforward way when doing a self-portrait. Because you are looking at a reflection you find yourself looking at a reflection of your hand holding up a viewfinder which obscures your face!

You are doubtless familiar with the standard joke of the artist (complete with smock and floppy Rembrandt hat) doing something peculiar by holding his arm outstretched with thumb upright in front of his subject. This is, in fact, a very useful measuring device, easier to do with a pencil than with your thumb. Your arm must be fully outstretched. If you bend your arm the change in the scale of the pencil, which you are using as a measuring stick, in relation to the subject is really dramatic. Test this to see for yourself. Making sure your arm is fully extended, hold the pencil upright and slide your thumb down it to measure the height of an object—a building in the distance or an object on the table. Say the height of the building measures half the length of your pencil. Keeping your thumb in the same place on the pencil, bend your arm so that the pencil comes toward you. With the arm bent, line the pencil up with the object that you measured. When your arm was fully stretched the building was perhaps half a pencil high. Now your arm is bent, the pencil is nearer and therefore looks larger. The building would now measure only one-quarter of the length of the pencil; your thumb, down at the halfway mark, is completely in the wrong place. This clearly demonstrates how, when you use this measuring device, you must always remember to keep your arm fully outstretched. All the measurements will then remain constant. During a drawing you use this aid to check the size of one thing against another.

Try this intriguing exercise to see for yourself how remarkable are the changes in scale in what we see. You'll need a piece of clear cellophane or acetate, some pieces of adhesive tape and a drawing medium that will adhere to the shiny surface of the cellophane or acetate. A few types of felt pen will do this, otherwise make a mixture of ink or poster paint and liquid detergent which you can apply with a brush. Fasten the cellophane or acetate to a window and draw, in outline, onto it, the objects you can see. To do this you will find it essential to close one eye. Each time you move, even a very little, the objects will slip out of their outlines, so you must carefully line them up again before resuming work. This is more difficult than you might think. It's most interesting to see how remarkably small familiar objects, that you know to be large, like houses, can actually appear. This is called 'drawing sight-size'.

Although you know that the lines are parallel, the two sides of this track across the desert seem to converge at the horizon. This is the basis of perspective.

Use the same principle when working from a still life group or a figure. We in fact rarely draw sight-size naturally. This time don't draw on a transparent material, use your normal paper. Endeavour to make your drawing absolutely the same size as you are actually seeing the subject. Measure frequently, using the pencil as a measuring stick, and the viewfinder device too, if you like. Before you begin the drawing it is wise to check the measurement of the total subject. If it is a standing model, and he or she appears to be only about 5cm (2in) high, you would be well advised to move in a little closer. Of course, don't get so close that the model is much longer than the pencil!

Perspective

While doing these sight-size drawings you will have become particularly aware of the way in which things, especially those objects whose form is based on a rectangular or cube-like shape, such as buildings, appear to be full of sloping sides and angles. This feature is perspective. This needlessly awe-inspiring subject is, in fact, only one method of conveying the idea of three-dimensional space on a two-dimensional surface. It is really a kind of trick and not an exact parallel of what we actually see. We see with two eyes—with binocular vision. As our eyes are spaced apart, we see a slightly different view with each eye.

Hold a matchbox up in front of you so that the narrow end, with the drawer, is facing you, and just a very little of the right-hand rough

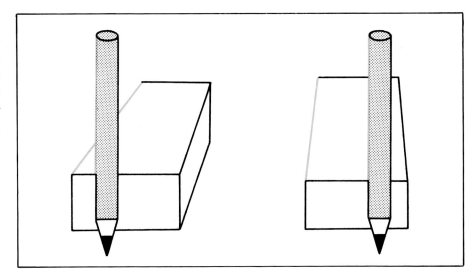

striking side visible. Hold it so that you can see it comfortably, without squinting. Now close your right eye. The striking side will disappear. You don't see that view of the box with the right-hand striking side with your left eye, which is now open, only through your right eye.

Now, with both eyes open, look at the long left-hand top edge of the box that is coming toward you. Alternately open and close left and right eyes, the whole box itself will appear to jump across a little each time. Observe the apparent change in the angle of the slope of that long left-hand side. When viewed through your left eye, the angle is much nearer the vertical than when it's viewed through the right eye. Hold your pencil up in front of the box to verify this. (Incidentally, watch how the position of the pencil in relation to the box mysteriously changes.) Fig. 3 illustrates this.

These simple tests demonstrate how we actually see slightly around the side of things with our own particular human type of binocular vision. This ability assists us in assessing the three-dimensional aspect of objects—how they come forward or recede.

The theory of perspective drawing was developed during the Renaissance. It is one of those subjects that has become cloaked in mystique, but the basic principles upon which it all rests are not difficult to understand. The theory assumes that you see through one eye only, remaining in a fixed position—just as you do when you make a sight-size drawing on cellophane. Normally when we look at a scene our eyes flicker all over it, gathering and assessing information. So drawing in perspective is like catching and freezing one phase of this scanning process, as if seen through one eye.

If you have tried the sight-size exercise on cellophane, you will know that it is not a very convenient way of working. It is also surprisingly difficult. You don't always have a handy window between the subject and yourself, and you certainly don't want to confine your materials to clear cellophane and an ink and detergent mixture. If you grasp the simple principles of perspective you can apply them wherever and with whatever you are drawing. Fig. 4 shows a woodcut print by Albrecht Dürer depicting an artist making a perspective drawing of a figure, using various aids. The procedure shown here is a natural follow-on from the clear cellophane drawing exercise, so do try something similar yourself. The artist placed a vertical glass screen between himself and the model. On it and the paper he painted an accurate grid of squares. He used the obelisk-like object in front of him on the table to line his eye up as his head was bound to move about while doing the drawing; this enabled him always to return to exactly the same position. He looked through the screen and he could see the way in which each piece of the model fitted within each square. He could then draw what he saw in the glass squares onto the squares on his paper.

The glass screen represents what is known as the *picture plane*. That would normally be an imaginary upright surface between the artist and what he is observing and drawing. In the case of the Dürer illustration the glass screen forms an actual, touchable picture plane.

When you look out of your single (for perspective purposes) eye, you perceive, in effect, a cone of vision radiating out from the eye. Fig. 5 is a simplified version of Dürer's artist who has substituted three apples, all of similar size, for his model. The lines radiating from his eye represents the lines of vision to each of the apples, passing through the picture plane (the glass screen).

The apples are arranged one behind the other, but not quite in a straight line. Were they in a straight line in front of the artist's eye,

Fig. 4 This woodcut by Albrecht Dürer shows an artist studying perspective. The screen between the artist and the model represents what is known as the picture plane.

apple C, because it is nearest to him, would appear largest and would obliterate the other two.

Where the lines of vision pass through the picture plane, they are, as it were, trapped on it to make the picture. Imagine yourself in the same room as Dürer's artist. You are looking straight at the apples from the viewpoint of Dürer himself. Each apple is more or less the same distance away from you and therefore each appears approximately the same size. From the viewpoint of the artist who is portrayed, they vary considerably in their distance from him. Apple C features large in his cone of vision and is shown as the tallest on the picture plane. Apples B and A diminish markedly.

Try a similar drawing yourself using tea cups, sugar cubes or any group of objects that are more or less equal in size and shape. As you go about, look out for the phenomenon too. See how the heads in a crowd diminish in size toward the back rows; how the pebbles on a beach merge from being distinct oval shapes into a texture in the distance.

The René Magritte painting (fig. 6) done in 1955, creates a delightful joke out of the conception of the picture plane.

Next, consider the eye-level. This is a horizontal line right across what you are looking at and across your drawing. It is literally at the level of your eye. If you squat down, your eye level goes down with you; stand on a ladder and it goes up with you. The earth's horizon always coincides with your eye-level. Note this in the Van Gogh drawing in fig. 7. The horizon/eye level is high up on the drawing. The straight line of the horizon is here interrupted by the irregular edge of the hills in the far distance. The artist was drawing from a high point—the title is *La Crau, seen from Mont-Majour*—looking across a wide valley. Imagine the flat, cultivated plane seen from the viewpoint of someone standing in the lane that slants across approximately the lower third of

Fig. 5. Distance alters the appearance of size as shown by this adaptation of Dürer's woodcut.

the picture. Their horizon/eye-level would be much, much lower down and consequently they would see far less of the fields laid out before them.

In the John Constable sketch of Salisbury Cathedral from the northwest (fig. 8), the artist is drawing positioned on the flat ground plane, not above the scene.

We have seen in the Dürer illustration how the lines of vision form angles for the eye to take in objects. The further away an object, in our

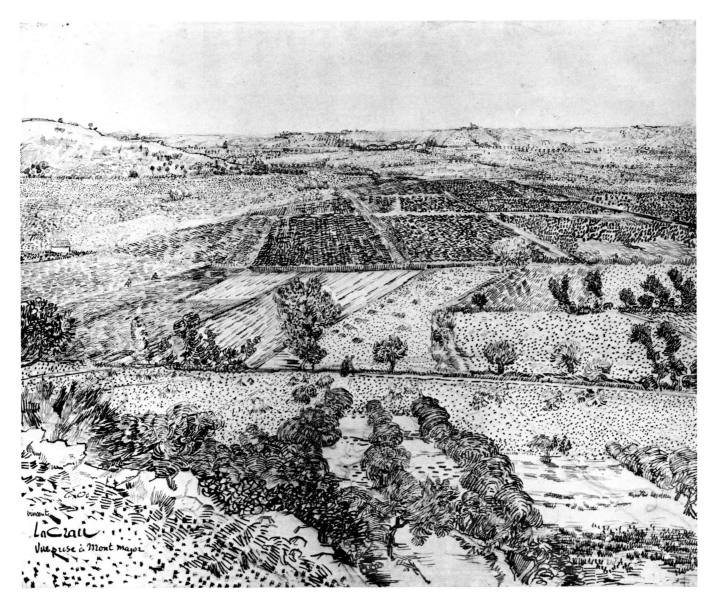

Fig. 7 La Crau, seen from Mont-Majour, *Vincent Van Gogh, pen and ink.*

example an apple, the narrower the angle becomes. If our artist were supplied with a great many more apples, all placed one behind the other on boxes of equal height to the original one, the apples furthest away from him would appear minute. If circumstances permitted, enough apples could be laid out so that the ones right at the back appeared so tiny he wouldn't be able to see them.

No doubt you have observed a similar phenomenon when looking at a long straight line of telegraph poles. You know they are all the same height and all equally spaced and yet they literally seem to disappear into the distance, getting smaller and closer together. The angles of vision through which you perceive each telegraph pole are getting narrower and narrower.

Any pair or more of lines that are parallel to one another will appear to converge as they recede into the distance. This is very apparent when looking down a rail track. The word 'line' here does not necessarily mean an actual visible line, but it can be an imagined line linking, for instance, all the bases or all the tops of the telegraph poles together. It can also refer to the edges of a surface or plane.

The place at which the parallel lines meet is called the *vanishing point*. Any parallel lines receding from the viewer (sides of a building, edges of a road, sides of a table), that are horizontal will always appear to meet at a vanishing point on the horizon/eye-level. These horizontal lines are always parallel to the ground. They can be on the ground like a roadway, or above or below the horizon like the sides of a building.

Fig. 8 Salisbury Cathedral from the Northwest with cottages, *John Constable, pen and bistre ink.*

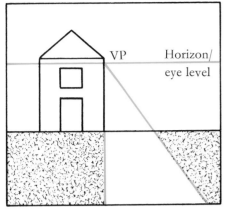

The diminishing effect does not apply to horizontal lines that are viewed parallel to the observer's eye; that is straight in front of you, as the apples that were straight in front of Dürer himself.

If you stood in the window on the first floor room of a building next door to this house, it would look like the drawing in fig. 9. The only perspective angles here are in the road. Move into a similar first floor window on the opposite side of the street and the angles immediately appear in the house (fig. 10). All the parallel horizontal lines can be seen to be extending to meet at vanishing points on the horizon/eye-level. The parallel lines of the sloping roof meet in a vanishing point way above the horizon. This is because the plane of the roof is not parallel to the

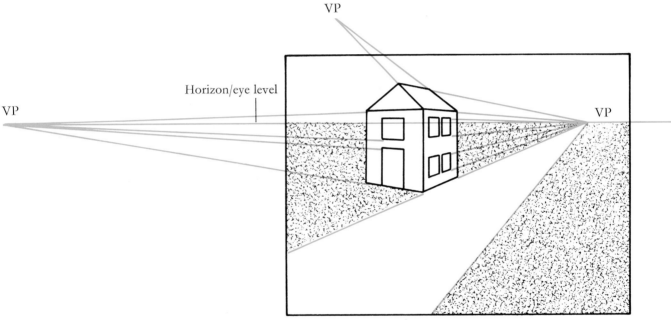

Fig. 9 (above), fig. 10 (right) In both drawings VP is the vanishing point. Fig. 11 far right, The Annunciation, Carlo Crivelli. Use a ruler to trace the lines in the composition back to the vanishing point. Although the painting is very complex there is only one vanishing point.

ground, but at a different angle. The vanishing points of such lines can be situated anywhere, that is, wherever they logically extend to and meet.

As you see, the vanishing points, whether of horizontal or other types of parallel lines, may well be outside the actual picture. If you need to, you can always add extra pieces of paper to help with your perspective construction.

Fig. 11, *The Annunciation,* painted by Carlo Crivelli in 1486, is a classic example of the use of perspective. In fig. 10 the house is viewed slightly from the side so there are two vanishing points of the horizon/eye-level. In Crivelli's picture, which at first glance looks very complex, the scene is represented from a straight-on viewpoint. Therefore there is only one vanishing point.

Look at the brickwork on the wall in the centre of the picture. The lines of mortar are all parallel and all horizontal (parallel to the ground). Find, with your ruler or a set square, the one that is actually horizontal on the picture. This is the one that coincides with the horizon/eye-level. Look across to the smaller scale bricks on the other side of the passageway. There you will also find a corresponding horizontal line. Above this, all the parallel lines that go back into the picture slope downwards toward the vanishing point. Below it, all parallel lines slope upwards to the vanishing point.

The lines between the paving stone upon which the angel and the

Fig. 12 In his pen and ink drawing of The Sea at Saintes-Maries, *Van Gogh uses several tricks to give an impression of depth: lines of diminishing size and variety and less detail on the distant boats.*

saint are kneeling obey the same rules. Follow the central one, which is vertical. The vanishing point lies where this line and the horizontal brickwork line intersect. The point is positioned in the bottom right-hand corner of the coat of the distant figure with a red hat. All the other horizontally parallel lines in the composition can be extended to meet at this point—even the steep edges of the roofs and the interior decoration of the ceilings on both floors.

Do have a good, long look at this picture—at the original in the National Gallery, London, if you can. In addition to the beautifully painted building it is full of wonderfully observed studies of still life groups, birds, sky and people, all considered in perspective, and thus contributing to the illusion of three-dimensional space.

The device of diminishing size to give the illusion of space can be used with any subject matter. As well as the possibly more obvious examples like buildings, it can be applied to textures or patterns. The Van Gogh landscape in fig. 7, again demonstrates this well. Similar drawn textures are used on the fields bordering the lane and on some of the fields way over in the distance. The scale of the texture is much reduced in the latter.

Objects nearer to the viewer not only appear larger, they also appear more clearly defined; detail is more evident; they are stronger in colour and more contrasting in tone too. Think of looking out to sea, especially on a mild hazy day. Standing by a boat that is lying on the beach you can see all its details, every nut and bolt, the grain of the wood, the texture of the seat. In a similar boat, some fifty yards out to sea, you will still be able to discern the colours quite clearly and know what the occupants are wearing. A craft much farther out will appear as a blue-grey silhouette shape. You'll probably be able to tell if there are one or two people on board but your eyes will be unable to give you any information as to the boat or the occupants' clothing. An object appears less distinct the farther away it is from you because there is more atmosphere between you and the object. See the Van Gogh drawing in fig. 12 for an illustration of this fact.

The types of marks we make in a drawing are largely governed by the medium being used. When wishing to convey an idea via a visual symbol—which is, after all, what drawing is about—the automatic action is to draw in line. Imagine you are on a holiday abroad and you cannot speak a word of the language. You are looking for a camping site. You accost a native and either with a ballpoint pen on a scrap of paper or with your finger in the sand you outline the shape of a tent. This is the basic drawing method—putting a line around something. The native will either get the message or not depending on how convincingly you have captured the shape. If he stands there looking vacant no amount of shading, however exquisitely applied, will help.

Fig. 13 Portrait of Stravinsky, *Pablo Picasso, pencil.*

Tents don't have lines around them, any more than human figures, or trees, or buses do. The line is an abstract convention and it is universally understood as such. Also, the line is a mark made spontaneously, as if it's instantly seen as being the way to convey an idea—think about this. It is totally automatic in handwriting, we are so very familiar with drawing the various letters in linear form (in line) that we don't think twice about it. We only stop to think how we are going to form the letters when we are faced with writing or printing in some unusual circumstances. This occurs, for example, when hand-lettering a notice or a poster or handwriting an important letter.

Writing is, however, putting a line around a flat shape. It is not concerned with representing the illusion of a solid object (or objects). How can line be used in this context? As with the tent example, an outline can produce a most telling image. But it is worth noting that it

is only certain views of an object that will convey the message so clearly in outline alone. It must be a view that succinctly sums up the character of the object, rather in the same way as a silhouette does. In many instances, a line around the outside alone would mean very little. An outline of a human head, with plenty of hair, facing toward you will give you much less information than a linear profile of the same person. Look out for trade marks, symbols and other examples of design that exploit the significant shape idea, either in outline or in silhouette form.

The various ideas mentioned in the section on perspective can all be brought into play in a line drawing. However, and this applies to whatever kind of drawing you are doing, it is no good simply applying a mechanical formula. That will produce a lifeless, mechanical drawing. You must study your subject and think your way around it; imagine what it feels like—in fact, let all those feelings that were discussed at the beginning of the chapter come flooding in.

Objects can be shown diminishing in size in a linear way. The actual nature of the line itself can also be changed and adjusted to suit what it is portraying. Its thickness and density may be altered. It can be made strong or tentative, definite or nervously dotted. With your own drawing materials see how many types of line you can make.

Objects, or parts of an object, can be shown to overlap and partially obscure other parts. This indicates that one thing is in front of another. It can also show that one thing is affecting another. This can be seen in the linear Picasso pencil drawing (fig. 13). The sitter's left hand is clearly near the viewer. The attitude of the hand (the way in which the outline correctly captures the shape) and the tension lines as the shirt sleeve is pulled down indicate a model slightly ill at ease. Look at his face—he doesn't look relaxed. Note the way in which, all in the minimum of lines of a similar weight, the left arm is shown to recede.

The fine Matisse self portraits (fig. 5 in the Project chapter) are drawn in a crayon line. During his very active working life, Matisse made many, many drawings from the figure. Frequently, he would make highly detailed studies, often of the same pose, several times over. He would be familiarizing himself with the form. This knowledge gave him the confidence to put down these rapid kinds of drawings, where shapes are sized up and expressed in such a pithy way. If you are unsure of the idea you are wishing to express you cannot put it down with such assured nonchalance.

As you think your way around, over and across the subject you will find that you are using line, this abstract convention, to explain different types of things. As we have seen, line not only goes around the edges of an object, it can go up and over it, following the contours.

It can be used to indicate an edge where one colour changes to another and where one plane meets another plane.

Tone

In his pen and ink drawing of a dazzling day at the sea (fig. 12), Van Gogh uses line technique in a way that builds up areas. This approach is rather like making a painting. One area is seen against another; all are seen as parts of the entire composition. The lines are massed together in their different ways to constitute the appropriate texture and the appropriate tone or weight for that section of the picture. In the foreground there is plenty of contrast between the heavy, tempestuous black lines on the white, making the waves sparkle and splash about. Going back toward the horizon the water is drawn in a series of gradually diminishing lighter, parallel, slightly wiggly lines with some white gaps. This part of the sea seems to shimmer. Amazingly enough, seen in this context, against this particular shimmering texture of the water and the intense white of the sails, lots and lots of little black dots read as a bright blue sky! The sails appear bright and white because they are surrounded on all sides by textures.

Here Van Gogh is using different weights, or tones, in his drawing to parallel, in black and white, the colours and the surface qualities of what he sees.

Tone, that is, areas of light and dark and all the grades in between, can be used in an infinite number of ways in drawing. An artist can employ tone to model the shape of an object, to give the illusion of its being three-dimensional.

The way in which light falls on an object has a profound effect upon explaining what that object looks like. Take a commonplace example: In the dusk it's difficult to recognize a person walking toward you, there is only a limited amount of light falling on that person—sufficient for you to know that it is a person and not a camel approaching you. Only when they step onto the lighted porch do you recognize them.

When you were setting up your self-portrait it was stressed that the lighting should remain constant. Natural light is extremely capricious, moving around all the time with the sun going in and out of clouds.

Here is a very useful exercise which really helps you to see how light explains the three-dimensional forms of objects. Gather together several white objects to set up in a still life group on a piece of white paper with a white background. Find something based on a cylinder, this might be a mug or a roll of paper; a spherical object, say a table tennis ball; and something cube-like, perhaps a white box. Use a drawing medium that you feel happy with as a tone-maker. This may be pencil, different grades can be used gently to construct tones, or charcoal, both perhaps worked in conjunction with an eraser which is also used as a drawing tool; brush and dilute ink—whatever you wish. Try to work with the minimum of lines. Use them only to construct (tentatively) and plan out the drawing.

Arrange your still life so that it is lit, more or less, from one side, as opposed to being lit from above. Place the objects so that parts of each of them are in front of the others. Make your drawing, using any of the measuring devices that seem applicable. The viewfinder will be especially useful here. Study the group carefully and compare how light or dark the parts of the objects are, one against another and against the white background and the white base. See how very much the tones vary, even on a flat piece of white paper. In some cases the lighted side of an object will appear to be much, much brighter than the background behind it. In other instances the reverse will apply. There will be reflected light catching the objects too. This is illumination, not from the main source, but reflected back onto the articles off the wall or the surroundings.

Remember that your white paper is the lightest tone you have at your disposal. Try to chart the different grades of tone there are in the whole group. Don't forget that, as in the Van Gogh sea picture, a white can appear extra white because it is isolated in the middle of several tones.

Upon reading this, the description of the contents of the still life may seem monumentally dull. However, as soon as you grasp the essential aim of the exercise you'll see that going right to the basics is vital. These forms, the cylinder, the sphere and the cube are the fundamental bases of all natural forms. They may be distended or compressed, the sphere may become egg shaped, the cube more rectangular—but everything can be sorted out to be seen to be based on these three forms. Do remember this when faced with a complicated object—the human figure for instance. The Luca Cambiaso pen and wash drawing in fig. 15 clearly shows him planning a composition with this sort of practice in mind. The drawing was done in the sixteenth century, but it presages the twentieth-century Cubists.

Having made your study with the light coming from one side, try some different lighting just to see how drastically the appearance of the still life group changes. Shine a flashlight on it, from different directions, in a darkened room. This produces stark, sharply contrasting results like dramatic theatre lighting.

Tone and line may, of course, be used together in a drawing, as in the Luca Cambiaso example, the Constable in fig. 8 or the Holbein in fig. 16. The use of tone alone in the exercise was to emphasize the point and to encourage you to look in a new way. Notice in the Holbein, as you will see in many other drawings, how the surface on which the hand is resting is indicated in tone. Objects are not seen in isolation but always in relation to other things. Even this slight suggestion places the hand in a three-dimensional situation.

Another intriguing project to try with your all-white still life group is interpreting it in colour. When you look long and hard at it you will see that the whites themselves vary considerably. The actual materials that

Fig. 15 (left) Group of Figures, *Luca Cambiaso, pen and wash.*

the different items are made of are all different kinds of whites. This is local colour, the basic, inherent colour of something. Some objects will be bluish-white, some creamish, some even pinkish. The tones of the shading on them are not merely shades of a nondescript, equal grey. There are all manner of subtle colours within the greys. Colour has a grammar of its own.

Try out some different kinds of linear interpretations of the group. These could be in colour too. Keep your basic still life forms and use them for exercises of your own devising.

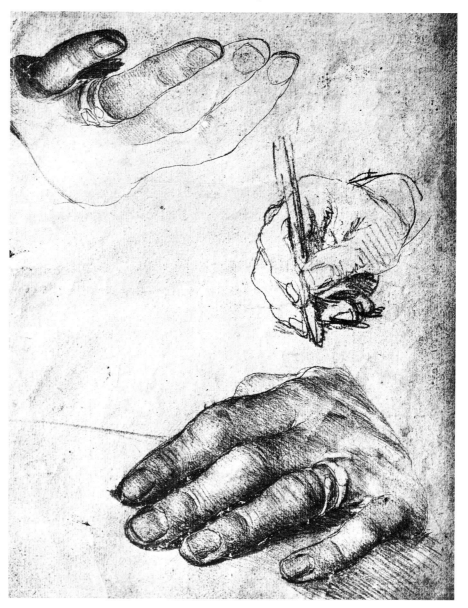

Fig. 16 Study of Hands, *Hans Holbein, pencil and red chalk.*

Improving Observation

Having looked at the constituent elements of the visual language, consider further how these elements can be used. Several examples are shown in this chapter which study either one particular element, or a group of them. Use these illustrations to stimulate your own ideas, trying a similar approach yourself, but not necessarily of the same subject matter or in the same drawing medium. Pick out certain elements and examine them closely in relation to your drawing.

The art student who did the drawing in fig. 1 has tackled perspective drawing by, first of all, marking out a grid of squares on the floor in masking tape. The furniture is then positioned randomly over the grid. In the Dürer perspective drawing shown earlier, the network of lines made a flat grid superimposed on the drawing. In these examples the grid is an integral part of the still life group. It, as well as the objects in the group, is seen to be receding and diminishing in size (perspective). You can sense that the parallel sides of the squares that go back across the floor would, if extended, eventually meet at a vanishing point.

The squares assist the artist in plotting the position of each article and in checking the scale of one item against another. Both drawings use a linear pencil technique.

Try a project of this kind yourself. Either set up your objects on an accurately constructed network of squares or use a suitable, already squared surface to serve the same purpose. Square tiles would be ideal—or a check tablecloth. Deliberately set out to draw what the spaces between the objects look like. You'll be looking at irregular areas, with on some occasions, the rigid divisions of the grid lines cutting across them.

Remember the suggestions for measuring and composing the drawing. Another useful aid to help you sort out what kind of an angle a line is lying at is to use a small, transparent 45° set square (this is the type with a right angle and two equal 45° angles). It is often very difficult to decide just how an angle is sloping or whether a line is actually horizontal or vertical. To check a line that is near the horizontal, hold the set square up in front of you and line the vertical side up with some subject you know to be vertical. In a landscape this might be the corner where the walls of a house meet. You'll be able to see, because the set square is transparent, whether the near-horizontal line coincides with the horizontal edge of the set square, or at what sort of angle it slopes up or down away from the horizontal. The same principle applies to near-vertical lines. In the same way, you can use the 45° angle to estimate the direction of similar types of angles. Is the line on the 45° line, halfway through the 45° angle, and so on?

The sensitive drawing in fig. 2, is another visual statement of a way of thinking that links up with the two previous drawings. A large and very varied still life was set up—all sorts of things. The idea in this project is to take the viewer for a walk across a section of the still life group; to follow a trail across it. The string that snakes around and over the objects and across the floor marks out the trail. Careful observation is called for to note the effect of perspective upon the objects and to see just how one

Fig. 1 (below) Upturned Stools, *Debbie McCarthy, pencil.*
Fig. 2 (right) Still Life, *Nicola Fredricks, pencil.*

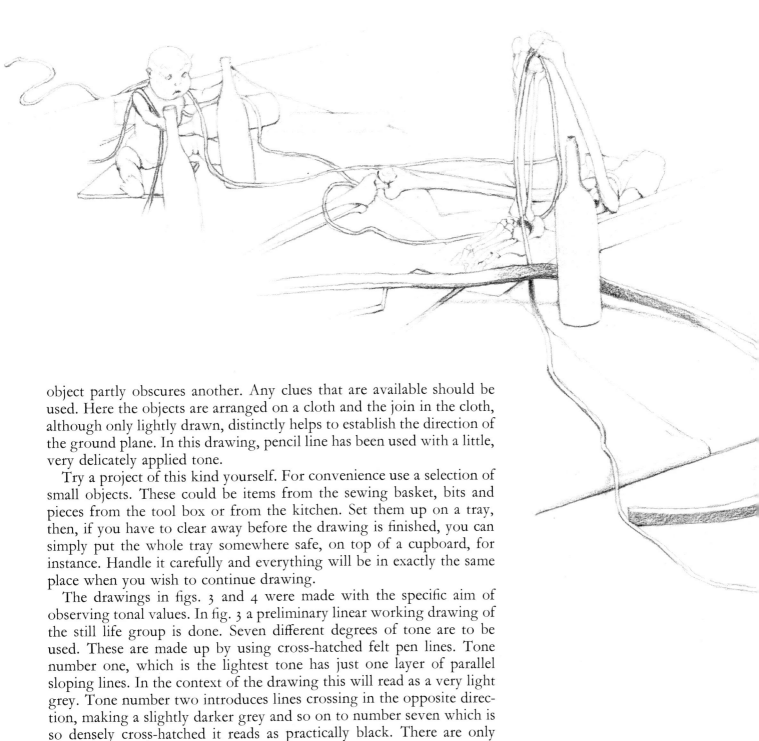

object partly obscures another. Any clues that are available should be used. Here the objects are arranged on a cloth and the join in the cloth, although only lightly drawn, distinctly helps to establish the direction of the ground plane. In this drawing, pencil line has been used with a little, very delicately applied tone.

Try a project of this kind yourself. For convenience use a selection of small objects. These could be items from the sewing basket, bits and pieces from the tool box or from the kitchen. Set them up on a tray, then, if you have to clear away before the drawing is finished, you can simply put the whole tray somewhere safe, on top of a cupboard, for instance. Handle it carefully and everything will be in exactly the same place when you wish to continue drawing.

The drawings in figs. 3 and 4 were made with the specific aim of observing tonal values. In fig. 3 a preliminary linear working drawing of the still life group is done. Seven different degrees of tone are to be used. These are made up by using cross-hatched felt pen lines. Tone number one, which is the lightest tone has just one layer of parallel sloping lines. In the context of the drawing this will read as a very light grey. Tone number two introduces lines crossing in the opposite direction, making a slightly darker grey and so on to number seven which is so densely cross-hatched it reads as practically black. There are only seven tones available in this exercise, so the objects must be carefully studied and decisions taken as to how the tones are to be distributed.

Applying a discipline of this kind, setting out to tackle a particular problem of observation and drawing interpretation is far more useful and informative than idly sketching with no real aim in view.

A coat hanger, seemingly most linear of subjects, is interpreted in fig. 5 completely in terms of tone against tone. As well as the changing values within the coat hanger itself the varying tones of the wall upon which it is hanging have been discreetly used to help describe the form. Because of the careful observation you can tell that this is a metal object against a flat matt surface.

From the range of drawings reproduced in this book it will be evident by now that subject matter is incidental. You can draw anything. Looked at with the attitude of an artist, any article is potentially interesting. New sensations, new sights are, of course, stimulating, but hurrying down to the south of France is not an essential prerequisite of the artist. What you see in the mirror, through your own window or in your own backyard can supply you with a profusion of material from which to work, now that you begin to know what you are looking for.

Traditionally artists have always made a practice of drawing from the

Figs. 3 and 4 Tonal Study, *Debbie McCarthy, felt pen.*

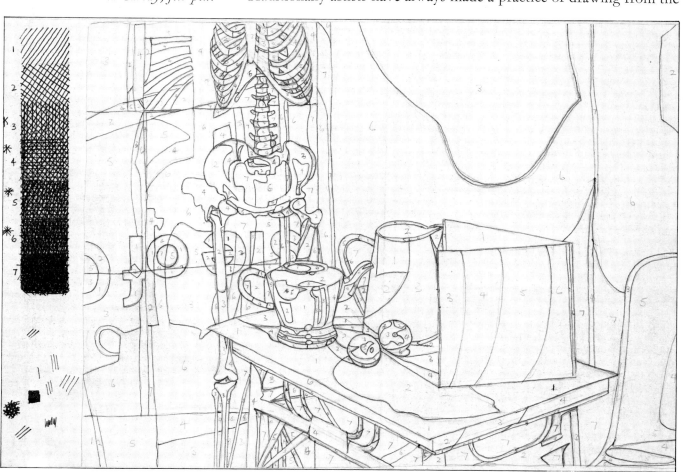

nude. Very probably they like nudes, but this isn't the sole reason. It is, once again, a case of getting down to basics. The clothing on a figure obviously obscures and disguises the form. If you can, try to get some experience of drawing from the nude. There may well be a life drawing class somewhere in your locality. Alternatively, a group of people who are interested in drawing and painting might club together and hire a model. If you simply can't obtain a life model perhaps someone would pose in a swimming costume; you will be able to see the structure of the body.

The local museum may have a human skeleton for you to study. Get an artist's anatomy book from the library and see how the muscles, etc. are fitted onto the basic framework of the skeleton. Have the book by you when you are drawing from the figure so that you can sort out why things look as they do.

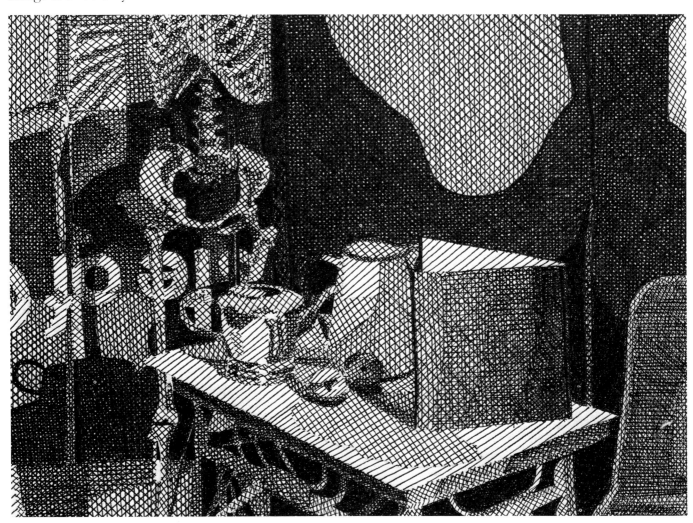

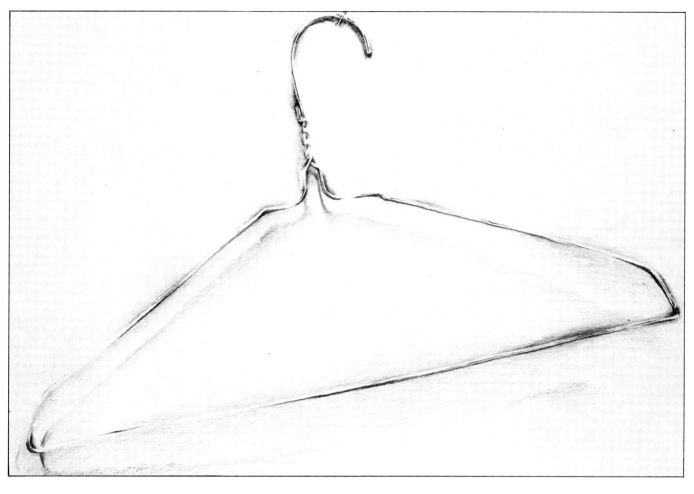

Fig. 5 Coathanger, *Hannah Hatchman, pencil*.

Try, if at all possible, to arrange for the same model to be available for a number of sittings. Use the time sensibly. Have a set pose for a drawing that is going to be worked on over a period of time. Use chalk to mark the position of the model's feet, hands and other relevant parts on the floor and also the furniture so that he or she can easily resume the pose after taking a break.

Use part of the session to make some quick drawings. Work in a medium that lends itself to producing rapid, immediate marks—perhaps charcoal or Conté. Or, like Rembrandt in this swift study of a sleeping girl (fig. 6), you could use a brush and wash. Ask your model to take up a pose for a very short time, three minutes, say. As the pose is brief it can be a more than usually energetic one. Do a number of these short pose studies, a new pose after every three minutes. Then, ask your model to walk around, perhaps repeating a movement like dropping a scarf and picking it up again. Draw as the figure is actually moving; this is an excellent way to train your visual memory. You will find you have to do a great deal of looking and careful observing. You have to fix a phase of the movement in your mind and then try to put the whole thing down on paper. When your memory fails you, pause for a second until the model again goes through the particular motion that you are studying, and watch out for the part that's eluding you. Try this same approach to drawing children and animals.

A great help in figure drawing is to think yourself into the pose. Imagine you were actually standing, leaning or sprawling like the model. Think which part of your body would be supporting your weight.

The Michelangelo drawing (fig.7) shows his skill in anatomy. The figure is under strain and the muscles are tensed and hard. It is

Fig. 6 Study of Sleeping Girl, *Rembrandt, brush, ink and wash.*

Fig. 7 (left) Study for the Libyan Sibyl, *and right, the completed fresco in the Sistine Chapel, both by Michelangelo.*

interesting to see how the use of the lighting conveys the rectangular space beyond the figure's head, enclosed by the upheld arms. Note also the various drawings of toes, etc. This is absolutely a working drawing, clearly demonstrating the process of discovery through observation.

As with any pursuit one can become quite complacent when drawing from the figure. There's always the danger of slipping into a comfortable way of drawing, of developing a reasonably successful formula and forgetting all about looking and observing properly. The next project, illustrated in fig. 8, gives such possible creeping complacency a shuddering jolt. A group of art students made self-portrait drawings on a massive scale. If you have a large enough room, you can try it too. A number of sheets of paper must be joined together and fixed to a suitable working area. A drawing medium of an appropriate scale is chosen, thick charcoal sticks or very soft pencils.

The artist must study his or her face in a looking glass, memorizing not only a particular feature or section, but how that section appears in relation to the whole. He then has to move away to work on the immense drawing surface, standing on a ladder, if necessary. He must keep standing back from the drawing to see it as a whole; to see if the various parts are being kept in proportion to one another and correctly positioned within the total framework. Manoeuvring tones and textures is vital too. Working on a scale where the drawing of the iris of your eye is actually the size of your own torso means you are looking at a familiar subject in a completely new way.

This same enquiring type of visual investigation can apply to anything. Of course, this doesn't mean everything must be drawn on a gargantuan scale! Next time you are cutting up vegetables, stop and consider them as potential drawing study material. The intricacies of the construction of a cabbage or cauliflower—this same relating of the parts to one another and to the whole—could provide a superb drawing subject. Flowers and plants offer a wealth of material too.

The fascinating idea behind the drawing by Hannah Hatchman in fig. 9 could be applied to a limitless selection of materials. The idea is to choose some objects with very different textural qualities and to try to

Fig. 8 Giant self portraits by the students of the West Surrey School of Art and Design.

represent these qualities in drawn form. The objects used here are feathers, fibreglass, a paper doily, fur fabric, and crumpled tissue paper.

In the same way as you think yourself into the model's pose, think your way around and over the objects in a still life group or a landscape. If it's feasible, walk around the subject so that you can get a more complete understanding of what it is like and how it is constructed. Remember how the cylinder, the cube and the sphere are the forms upon which all objects are based. Thinking of this can help in sorting out apparently amorphous things like clouds and trees.

Draw as much as possible from the real thing although drawing from photographs is sometimes necessary. For instance, you may need some

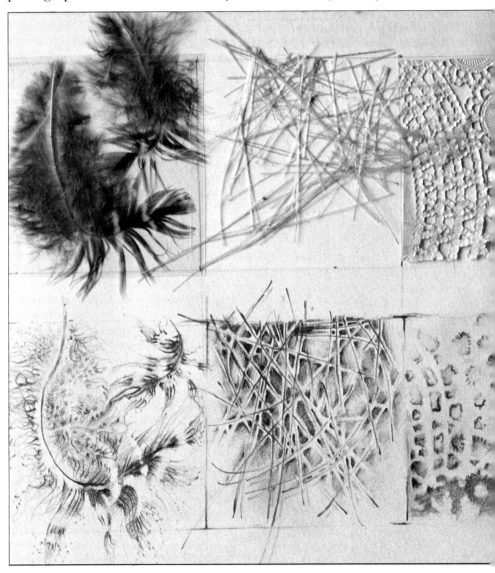

photographic reference for an object that is unobtainable. What a photograph can give you is always limited, compared with your direct experience of the object. A photograph is only one single view. There is no chance to walk around and see the thing from different points of view. Also the photograph is, as it were, some other person's way of transferring the three dimensional into the two dimensional. You have not been in control at all.

Endeavour to bring the elements of the visual grammar all together in your drawing. This is, obviously, no easy task. Clearly, as with any pursuit, the more you practice it, the better you become. Do THINK about your drawing. Give yourself a specific project or aim so that you

Fig. 9 Texture studies by Hannah Hatchman, pencil.

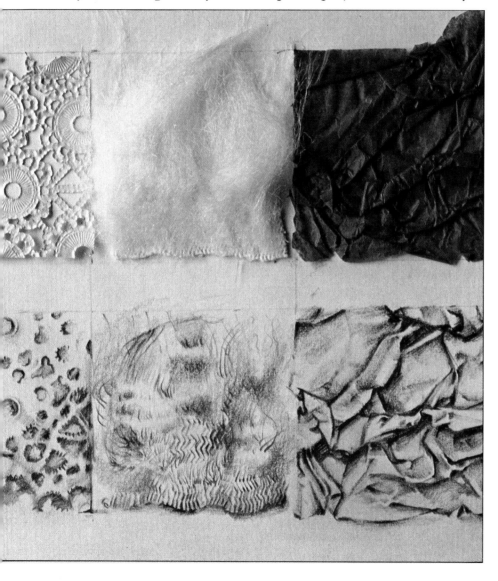

have a definite direction in which to work. As you progress, increase the number of aims within your projects. Consider how many factors Degas was dealing with in the coloured pastel drawing in fig. 10.

Date and keep all your drawings. You will then be able to chart your progress. Do also make written notes, even only the odd sentence about what you are endeavouring to achieve and how successfully—or otherwise—you have fared. Analyzing your progress in this way helps you to sort out what you are doing logically. Discussion with other people who are also involved in drawing and the visual arts will stimulate ideas, and looking at original drawings in museums and galleries is invaluable. You can approach them now to see how other artists have handled what you yourself are working with.

Fig. 10 Before the Mirror, *Edgar Dégas, pastel.*

A Techniques

The idea behind showing examples of different artists' work is not to urge you to copy a particular method of doing, say, noses. Rather it is to demonstrate the diverse ways in which the various drawing media may be used. Seeing examples of how ink, crayon and so on have been employed stimulates you actually to get hold of the materials to try them out for yourself. In your own drawing experiments, enjoy and savour the many techniques.

You need to establish a rapport with your materials. Observing what you are drawing and noting it all down is complicated enough, without the added difficulties of struggling with a seemingly recalcitrant medium.

Experiment with your drawing tools and the paper you intend to use before you begin a drawing. In this way you'll start discovering the possibilities and the limitations of the materials. If scratching with a pen

Reclining nude, *Hannah Hatchman, pencil. Here the pencil point has been used to make clearly defined lines and the side of the lead used to introduce areas of tone. Experiment with your tools and discover the many ways in which they can be used.*

is your metier, you will find out how hard you can scratch on a particular type of drawing paper from light- to heavy-weight, without actually tearing through. Maybe you need a tougher paper—an H.P. watercolour paper for instance. If you are using a lot of very fluid washes combined with, perhaps, a felt pen line, stretching the paper before you start may prove useful, to prevent it cockling badly.

Whatever the medium you are using, try out a good selection of different types of lines and tones. Use the drawing tool to make as many experimental marks as you can—tentative, delicate, fine lines; strong, heavy lines; wiggly lines; straight lines; thick lines made with the side of a crayon (these can shade from the hardly perceptible to the intense). Lay one colour across another too. If the medium is suitable, try out various smudging, blending and eraser-drawing techniques.

Pen and ink

Looking at some Van Gogh drawings may well inspire you to try using ink and a pen. In Materials you will find instructions for making a reed pen from bamboo, such as Van Gogh would have used; but any pen with a flexible nib will do. The spontaneous vitality, which is so much a hallmark of all Van Gogh's work, is clearly demonstrated in the pen and ink drawing of La Crau, seen from Mont-Majour (fig. 7, Elements of Composition). This spontaneity could never have been achieved if the artist had first meticulously drawn the scene in pencil and then gone over the pencil lines in ink. This is not to denigrate such a method (although simply 'going over' is questionable), merely to state that it does not lend itself to producing a spontaneous result.

Perhaps you would like to try drawing a landscape? This fascinating occupation combines the pleasure of being outdoors with that of making an entirely personal record of the places you visit.

So, you are all set up, comfortably seated in front of your view, armed with pen and ink—and with a glaring piece of white paper staring starkly at you. A flutter of nerves is inevitable but try not to panic. Don't draw anything until you've had a good, long look at the landscape. Use your viewfinder to select which bit you are going to do. The very act of looking through this enclosing frame is one definite step toward getting things under control. At least now, instead of fifteen square miles, or whatever it may be in your sight, you can actually hold in your hand the area you want to draw.

Look through your viewfinder and consider things at some length. Is the section you have elected to draw the same proportion as your piece of paper? If not, it's a good plan, at this point, to draw onto the paper a rough outline of an area that corresponds to the proportion of your chosen view. Whereabouts in the view does the horizon fall? The main line of this can be lightly indicated on your paper. In a similar way, look

Fig. 1 Madonna and child with cat, *Leonardo da Vinci, pen, ink and wash.*

86

at, check the position of, and lightly draw in the main features of the landscape. Look for decisive lines and divisions made by roads, hedges or a river, dominant blocks of buildings, clumps of trees and rocks. Lightly map all this in. Don't get bogged down at this stage with the fascinating details of a tree's branch or the intriguing patterns in its bark. Save these up as little treats for later on. The aim is to keep the complete drawing in balance all over so that it progresses, as far as is possible, at a similar pace throughout. Getting involved in one particular area, or with one object, however fascinating, in the early stages of a drawing is rather dangerous. The reasons for this danger are that you may well over-emphasize that object in terms of too much detail or too heavy a tone. It will be difficult and also illogical to bring the rest of the drawing up the same degree so that that specially-favoured piece doesn't stand out like a sore thumb. Also, having spent a good three hours working it up to perfection, you may find that it is in the wrong place!

While making sure you keep the weights, that is, the tones and textures of the different parts of the drawing in balance, think how, with your black ink and variable pen line, you can interpret the diverse qualities of the landscape. It is like a game. You must obey the rules— recording what you can see accurately without cheating—but at the same time, it's your individual interpretation of the rules that counts, coupled with the way in which you wield your drawing tool. Be as inventive and as ingenious as you can with it. Have some scrap paper handy on which to try out different kinds of marks. If you wish to experiment with a little area of texture to represent, for instance, a hayfield, draw it on the scrap paper, tear it off and hold it in the appropriate place over your drawing. This will show you if that kind of mark is too regular and mechanical, too heavy in tone or too large in scale. It may be helpful to do just a bit of one textured or patterned area and then bits of the ones adjacent to it. This again helps you to keep the whole drawing related and balanced.

This attitude toward drawing should apply regardless of the subject matter. Keep the whole thing, all the various parts, in balance; whether it be a picture of a still life, a figure drawing, a close-up study of a plant or a densely peopled composition like a battle scene.

If you draw something wrongly, and it becomes apparent to you as you progress with the drawing that it is wrong, draw over it. Re-do it in the right place or alter its construction. This conviction of your having understood what you were looking at, and of having appreciated the form of an object and its place in relation to the rest of the things in the drawing, will come shining through. Never mind about the fact that it is not so neat any more. You are merely rephrasing, more explicitly what you want to say, as you would do in the course of a verbal conversation. If you want strongly enough to say something you might initially

Fig. 2 Sketches of a child with cat, *Leonardo da Vinci, pen and ink.*

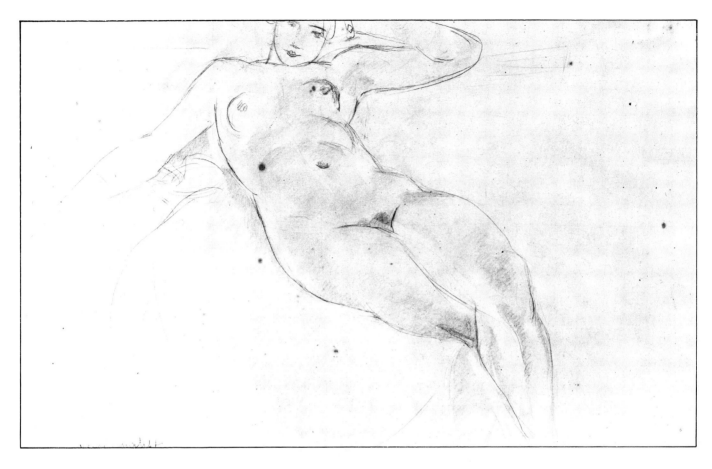

Etude de nu allongé, *Henri Matisse,*
charcoal. Using the charcoal to
establish line and tone, the artist
then erased some of the marks to give
highlights to the figure.

stammer it out, but ultimately you'll restate it so that there can be no doubt as to your meaning.

Freedom of expression is a thing so often advocated in books on art. Going out to search for freedom is a useless exercise; you are so self-conscious that it is the last thing you will find. Drawing in the way suggested here you may encounter it, without your realizing it at all.

The Leonardo da Vinci pen, ink and wash drawing in fig. 1 (so modern looking although it was done in the fifteenth century) demonstrates the restating process at work. The drawing is actually traced through from the pen and ink sketch which is on the other side of the paper—so much for any sort of reverence and preciousness! In the first drawing he's clearly had several different ideas about where the Madonna's legs should be. With the second version he has tried out, and settled for, a new position for her head: the drawing of her arm is greatly improved, it now tenderly supports the child. Christ sits much more securely in his mother's lap and the whole group is made to appear more solid by the addition of the cheerfully applied washes. It is interesting to note that this drawing is designed within a niche-shape, not a rectangle.

88

Fig. 3 The Wagnerites, *an opera-house audience, Aubrey Beardsley, pen and ink.*

With objects on the move, drawing over previously drawn lines is almost inevitable. No animal or child is going to remain stationary for any length of time (even if asleep). The lovely Leonardo quick pen sketches in fig. 2 show how the importance of getting it down on paper overrides anything about neatness, or fussing with the technique. Leonardo would have used a quill pen, which is even more flexible than a reed pen.

Aubrey Beardsley, the well-known Victorian illustrator, used pen and ink with a specific purpose in mind. His illustrations were to be reproduced by the line block process. This photo-mechanical method reproduces only black and white, no intermediate greys of any sort.

Thus Beardsley became highly skilled in getting the maximum out of black and white. Sometimes he would use large areas of white with very fine detailed black line drawing plus the occasional accent of solid black.

Fig. 3 is a fine example of Beardsley's skill. Here the same material, drawing ink, is used to produce a drawing in complete contrast to the previous examples. The use of huge areas of solid black makes the composition really dramatic—these would be inked in with a brush. The details of the architecture and the sly caricatures of the exclusive opera house clientele are pen drawn. Beardsley usually drew the composition roughly in pencil first and then, over the top of this sketched layout, drew meticulously with pen and ink. Notice the odd isolated area of texture, like the blond hair in among the black and white masses. Look too at the reverse use of the medium—white lines on black.

Fig. 4 Window and Rock, *Steve McMahon, pencil.*

If you are drawing in this sort of technique, watch yourself to see that, having done the initial pencil drawing, you don't just mindlessly ink over it. Use the pencil as a tool for mapping out the composition, constructing and working things out. Then, with just as much concentration, draw with the pen using it to elaborate details in the subject and convey tones by varying the thickness and types of line. Look again at the objects of your preliminary sketches and work from them as you use the pen and ink. Allow the pencil drawing to act merely as a guide. There is nothing so dead as a thoughtlessly inked-over pencil drawing.

The pencil drawings shown here demonstrate the enormous possibilities of the medium. Aside from the purely technical aspects, each drawing—as with all drawings—conveys its own distinct mood.

Fig. 5 Rhododendron, *Graham Rose, pencil.*

Pencil

Steve McMahon, who made the drawing in fig. 4 draws with an extremely hard pencil, a 6H or even a 7H, on good quality white drawing paper. He enjoys and exploits the way such a hard pencil actually carves a groove in the paper. Having drawn a line, one can shade up to it, the groove automatically stopping the shading lines and giving the area of shading a clearly defined edge.

The drawing in fig.5 by Graham Rose was done on smooth drawing paper using HB, 2B and 6B pencils. Two other pencil drawings on drawing paper from the same group of students are the townscape by Hannah Hatchman (fig. 6) and the tube by Jane Thoday (fig. 7). In the drawing of the tube, 2B and 4B pencils were used and this smooth type of shading was achieved by rubbing the pencil marks with a finger. Whites, as on certain of the ridges, were drawn in by erasing the pencil marks.

In the townscape the edge of a rock in the foreground forms a natural boundary for the drawing. An HB pencil has been used throughout. Drawings were being done in pencil as early as the fourteenth century. In those days, the pencil, sometimes known as stylus, was a solid rod of metal—zinc, lead or silver. The wooden casing was introduced later. Later still came the graphite-clay mixtures giving the wide range of pencils we now use.

These early instruments required a paper with a tooth to which the traces of metal could adhere as the pencil was drawn across it. Artists had their own particular methods of preparing the surface or ground with mixtures of, for example, chalk and gum. They would also frequently colour the ground. The Leonardo da Vinci study of hands

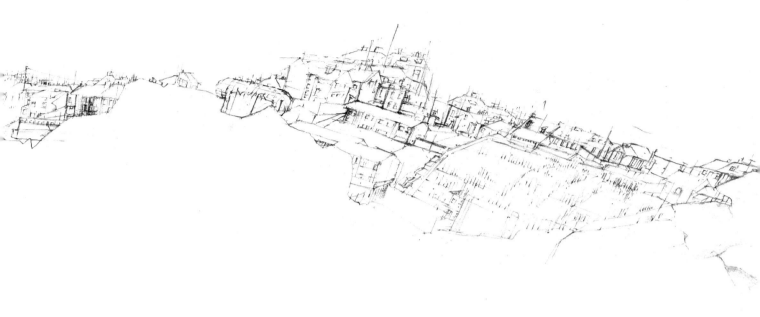

Fig. 6 Townscape, *Hannah Hatchman, pencil*.

(fig. 8) is done in silver point (a silver stylus) on a pink-coloured prepared surface. White drawing in chalk is added too.

A coloured or toned ground means the background starts off halfway, or some of the way, as it were, along the scale of tones. You can then draw marks that are lighter or darker than the background. With a white background you start at one end of the scale and you can only add darker marks.

The Leonardo silver-point drawing of a soldier in the full uniform of the time (fig. 9) is done on a prepared cream-coloured ground. It is rather unusual to see such a finished-looking drawing by this artist. Generally his drawings are clearly preparatory work for paintings, sculptures or the construction of machinery; or they are of the analytical, exploring kind, like his plant and anatomical drawings. Perhaps here he just got carried away by sheer enjoyment of the drawing techniques?

One of the greatest of innovators, Picasso, made the highly delicate pencil portrait of Max Jacob in 1917 (fig. 10) three years prior to the other, purely linear, portrait (fig. 13, Elements of Composition). These two examples demonstrate, once again, how versatile a familiar drawing instrument can be, even in the same hand.

Pastels

Pamela Day, who did the oil pastel drawing in fig. **11**, works on a fairly large scale. Oil pastels lend themselves to this broad, painterly approach. Contrast this with the technique of Delacroix's pastel drawing in fig. **12** where little dashes of colour have been used.

It's a good idea to keep a rag handy to wipe the tips of oil pastel sticks. As you draw one colour over another, the second stick picks up some of the first colour. So when you start drawing again that colour may be badly dirtied.

Experiment by combining pastels with liquid for some exciting combined drawing, wash and painting results. Use a brush and water for ordinary pastel, either before, after or during the drawing process. This does, in fact, make the colours less likely to smudge, but it is best to fix them anyway to be on the safe side. In a similar way, add white spirit (or turpentine—white spirit is less expensive) to oil pastels and to oil crayons. Have two small containers, as you do for oil painting; one with spirit to wash the brush in, and the other kept clean and used for diluting and mixing with the pastel colours. Consequently, the colours on the paper stay cleaner and you don't waste the white spirit. With water, whether with the pastel technique or when using ink washes, use just one container for both functions. The water will remain clean for a considerable time. Simply renew it as necessary.

In any painting technique, cultivate the habit of rinsing your brush frequently and drying it off on a rag after rinsing. This means you avoid splodging a lot of diluting liquid into the next colour. Pick up on the brush just the amount of liquid you mean to use.

Fig. 7 (below) Tube, *Jane Thoday, pencil.*
Fig. 8 (right) Study of Hands, *Leonardo da Vinci, silver point with chalk.*

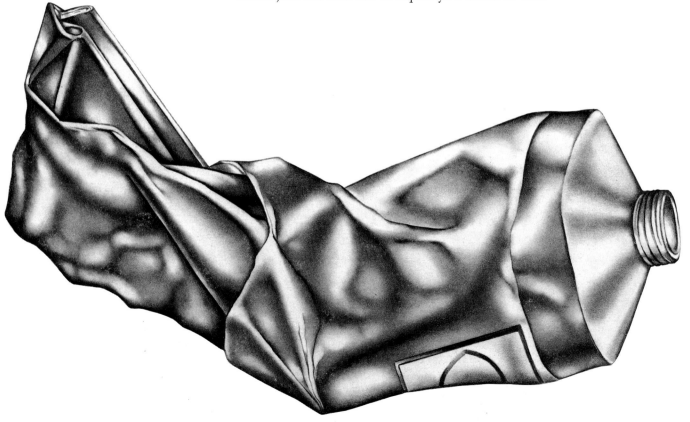

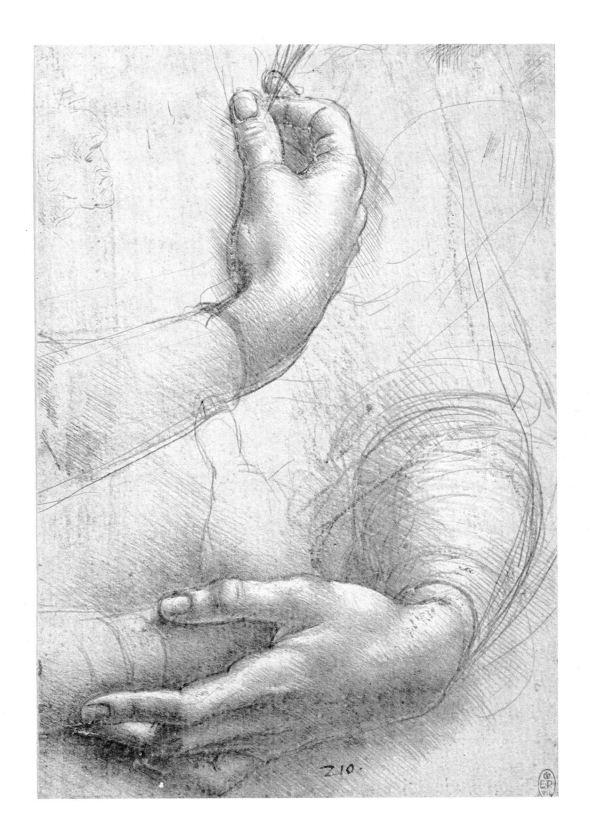

95

Resist drawing

As you know, grease and water don't mix. This fact can be exploited in what is known as resist drawing. Use oil pastels, wax crayons or an ordinary candle to draw in the parts that are to act as a resist. Paint watercolour or ink over the drawing. The previously waxed areas will not accept the liquid colour. Henry Moore, the sculptor, often uses this technique to draw in the light areas when representing three-dimensional objects. Fig. 13 is an example of his use of the technique.

Fig. 9 (right) Warrior wearing Helmet, *Leonardo da Vinci, silver point.*
Fig. 10 (above) Portrait of Max Jacob, *Pablo Picasso, pencil.*
Fig. 11 (far right) Children's party, *Pamela Day, oil pastel.*

Fig. 12 Study for Algerian Women,
Eugène Delacroix, pastel.

If you add a drop of liquid detergent to ink (or water paint) it will adhere to a waxy surface. In this way you can prepare a ground for the *sgraffito* technique. Use a stout paper or cardboard and crayon thickly all over it. Then cover it with the ink-detergent mixture. When this has dried you can scratch through the layer of ink to produce a clear, precise line in the crayon colour (or colours). Make yourself a scratching-drawing tool by inserting a sewing needle in a lead holder or a cork. Try out other tools too for different qualities of line—the blade of a craft knife, a nail, a small screwdriver, etc. This can produce quite a colourful result, like the drawing in fig. 14.

Felt pens

The two children's book illustrations shown in fig. 15 were drawn originally in different types of felt pens and markers. The first actually shows the child how to do the felt pen and wash technique. Obviously,

here you must use non-waterproof felt pens. Wet the paper first to achieve the irregular, blotchy effect. Alternatively, introduce water with a brush as the drawing progresses, to create washes and subtle shading.

In the second illustration fine pointed pens were used for the brown outlines and for the yellow ochre wood grain. The clay was coloured with two different tones of beige markers with thicker nibs. The darkest beige tones were achieved by several coats of colour. With certain pens and markers it is necessary to allow a colour to dry before going over it

Fig. 13 Detail of The Pink and Green Sleepers *from the Shelter Sketchbooks, Henry Moore, wash and wax resist.*

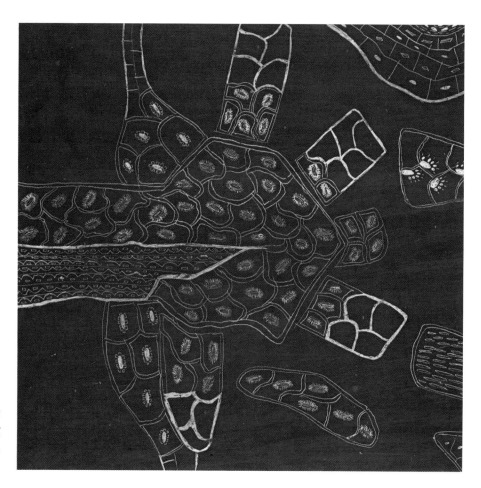

Fig. 14 Study of Cells, *Martin Harris. This child's drawing makes use of the* sgrafitto *technique, a type of wax resist drawing.*

again, thus avoiding scuffing up the paper. Also, with some makes of pen, adjacent colours will *bleed* (run) when wet and some felt pens may bleed on certain kinds of paper. Clearly you need to experiment first to find these things out.

Experiment by combining different media. There are no hard and fast rules as to what goes with what.

The glorious freedom that some of the drawings of the great artists achieve comes from the confidence and assurance of years of observing and practising. This same assurance, summing-up and judgement, this making of decisions and going into action can be seen expertly performed in all spheres of life. The star tennis player or golfer brings to bear all his knowledge to make the incredible winning stroke; the engineering craftsman or the chef performs his task eloquently with a finesse resulting from years of experience.

Clearly a beginner, because of his lack of experience, cannot expect to draw with this fluent confidence but he can admire and emulate the masters.

Extending the range

The more drawing you do the more your skills will improve, and consequently the greater your enjoyment will be. If you approach your subject in a thoughtful way, the more you draw the greater the number of facets you will begin to tackle. Sometimes, however, the process may feel to be anything but enjoyable; but this will not matter if you know the sort of thing you are trying in your own mind to sort out. At these frustrating periods your dexterity is lagging behind your ideas. The two, dexterity and ideas, go along inseparably hand-in-hand. Drawing, which at first you may have thought meant merely learning a few neat tricks that would enable you to put passable representations of things on paper, can lead the mind along all manner of avenues. Drawing is a process of enquiry, so it stimulates the mind. Take up drawing seriously and you will find your life enriched.

You may enjoy doing drawing for its own sake or you may wish to become more proficient at it as a means to aid some other creative pursuit. The ability to put down ideas in a visual form, i.e. to draw, is the foundation of many creative processes. The faculty of drawing is indispensable to virtually any kind of visual artist. Anybody who works in a design media uses drawing at some stage in the development of an idea. Consider the architect, engineer, painter, sculptor, couturier, stage designer and graphic artist. Drawing is the only logical way in which they can give form to and clarify their own thoughts. It is the means used to convey their message to others—both the final consumer and the intermediary craftsman. The architect must communicate visually with the builder and the client; the engineer with the tool-maker and the client; the couturier with the pattern cutter and the client.

The sketchbook and notebook

Cultivate the habit of carrying a sketchbook or notebook about with you. In this way you can jot down your observations in visual and written form. Some types of school exercise books are particularly suited to the writing and drawing form of notemaking as they have alternate plain and lined pages. You can always insert a stiff cardboard support inside the back cover.

The odd half hour spent in, say, waiting for a train can be profitably filled by using your sketchbook. Study your fellow travellers, the station itself, reflections in the waiting room window, a pigeon wandering up and down the roof, details of the architecture—anything that interests you.

Drawing in a sketchbook is frequently an impromptu affair and so it calls for instant mark-makers. On the station platform, with your train imminent, tidying up bottles of coloured inks, palettes, a water pot and brushes would seem hardly appropriate. Much more suitable would be

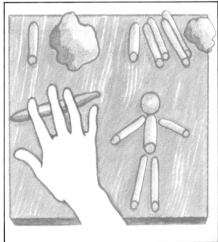

Fig. 15 These book illustrations were done in non-waterproof felt tip pen.

WINGED
SEAT.

ADJUSTABLE
STRAPS.

HINGED BACK SUPPORT.

one or two pencils in different grades (one with an eraser tip), thus giving a range of possible tones and lines, or a felt pen or two. Apart from the convenience of such drawing tools, there may be occasions, as when drawing the person sitting opposite you, when you wish to remain inconspicuous.

The sketchbook/notebook can become a fascinating illustrated diary. Quite aside from your using it to improve your skills in drawing and general observation, it makes a most interesting and entirely personal record of your past experiences. Use your sketchbook as an adjunct to your other drawing and related activities, but don't confine all of your drawing to it. Were you to do this you could become so used to the sketchbook page size, the particular type of paper it contains and those drawing materials that you become quite sluggish. For a healthy approach vary the size of the drawing, the location and subject matter and the drawing technique as you would vary your diet.

Written notes are very helpful to you, working in conjunction with your drawn information. It is often useful, when starting a drawing, to write down, simply in the form of a list, the things that strike you about the subject you are studying. Endeavour to elucidate what your aims are.

Make it clear to yourself, and there will be a good chance of making it clear to others via the drawing. Referring once again to the still life group previously shown (Elements of Composition) you might note how the whole atmosphere of this particular selection of objects conveys a feeling of well-being, the feeling is one of relaxation and leisure. Many of the shapes and patterns appear to echo this unhurried voluptuous theme. Rounded fruits (the pears have a look reminiscent of the slightly overweight), the elipses of the bowls, the glass, the lampbase and the cheeseboard, the wood grain of the tabletop, the wallpaper design—form comfortable curves. Sharp and jagged angles, which are the signals of movement and action, are absent here.

Early civilizations used pictures to record the history of their cultures. This rather gory scene is a page from a manuscript recording the Aztec practice of human sacrifice to the gods of their religion.

Look at the rich tonal contrasts. In some areas, for instance the bottles and the grapes, the definition of the forms on the unlit side is lost in the heavy shadows.

Are you using colour? For the initial mapping out perhaps a gold/ sienna or soft greyish-purple? Secondary colours are much in evidence here. Pure primary hues, which suggest a more active feeling, are almost absent. Most of the colours are muted, so try using the complementary mixing methods to achieve these subtleties. Don't, however, allow the colours to become turgid. Although they are not bright in the way primaries are, they are rich and glowing. Retain clarity as in the orange and green of the fruit.

All this helps you to clarify to yourself what you are doing. As the drawing progresses and you make new discoveries, jot them down too. This is especially practical if you are engrossed in a certain aspect of the drawing, and you don't wish to stop working on it when a particular thought enters your mind. Just a single word written down will remind you to consider that additional idea later on.

If you are drawing in monochrome—perhaps a quick sketchbook study—a written note of the important colours of the objects may prove useful, particularly if the drawing is to be used as preparatory work for a painting, illustration, etc. Similarly, notes on the effect of the type of light that prevailed at the time and the quality of the atmosphere all help to build up the picture. Occasionally, time and circumstances may not permit you to get all you want to down on paper in drawn form, but little written clues will help recapture it. Was the landscape looking brilliant and pristine after a sudden shower; was everything clearly defined with crisp edges; or were shapes merging as the misty autumn evening approached? All the time this kind of 'open-minded' attitude sharpens your powers of observations. You begin to discover things you never thought existed; colours in shadowed areas that had formerly just looked grey, and delightful contrasts of shapes and textures in the everyday things around you. Faces in a crowd will become fascinating. How marvellous are the amazing, endless permutations on the two eyes, nose and a mouth formula in colour, texture and proportions. Consider how you can use all these elements.

You will find yourself planning how you would arrange things in a drawing, what part of the view you would choose, what medium would seem suitable, how much space you would leave around the outside edge—would you make that section as dark in tone as this one—and so on. In short, you are creating compositions in your mind.

Even if you are passionately interested in one particular subject, try to vary the range of the things you draw, simply in order to refresh yourself. Do think about this. It is so easy to become stale. Have bad weather conditions meant that you've been forced to work entirely

Male Nude, *Angelo Visconti,*
chalk. This drawing illustrates how
when the weight is shifted, the
normally horizontal lines of the
shoulders, waist and hips assume
acute angles. Watch for this when
drawing from a model as it will help
you to get the figure correctly onto
the paper.

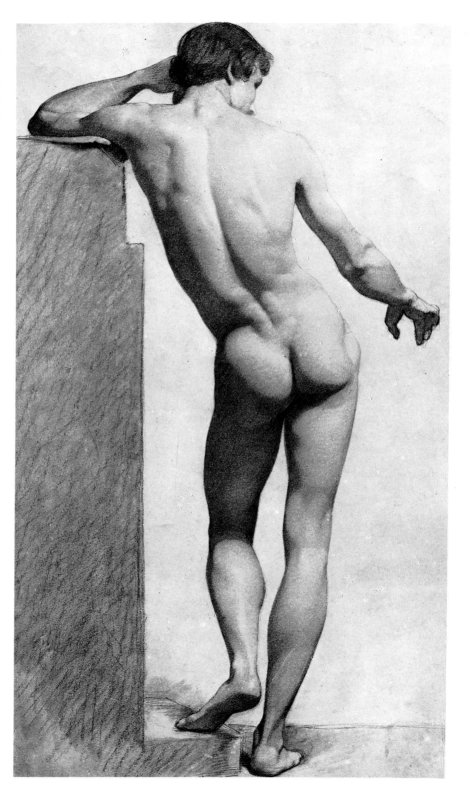

indoors for rather too long? Is your still life getting very dusty and, frankly, boring? Have a total change. If it's still too cold and wet for outside work what about a visit to the zoo, an aquarium or the glasshouses at a horticultural garden? (Check first, sometimes you need permission to draw in these places, so a preliminary telephone call is advisable).

If you've been immersed in huge rolling landscapes for quite some time, up to your ears in charcoal, perhaps a little close work would be a welcome alternative? Try some close-up studies of intricate plants or sections of plants, shells, jewellery or small articles with very differing qualities. How, for example, do you set about drawing such unlikely articles as a cupful of flour, a spoonful of sugar, some raisins and some dried lentils? (Think how you would set that up; what sort of background would you use?) This is the curious kind of problem that confronts the artist in the advertising world.

A total change of subject matter will make you think about what medium to use too. Never stop experimenting. Combine several mediums in the same drawing if that's the way you can explain what you want to say.

The same principles of drawing are applicable whatever the subject matter may be. Some subjects, of which figure drawing and plant drawing are two examples, are, unfortunately, classed as distinct and somehow special undertakings. This suggests that they have certain rules and know-how peculiar to themselves. This is not the case. Anything, any object, will serve as a subject to be drawn. Figures and plants are objects too. Exactly the same form of approach, the same method of enquiry can be exercised whatever the article that is being studied.

When working from the human figure as a drawing subject, some elementary knowledge of basic anatomy is required. This does not mean that you have to know all the Latin names for the bones and muscles (unless, for some other specific reason, you need this information). Being the possessor of a human figure you certainly have some understanding of how the body is constructed and how it moves. With the aid of a book that shows the skeleton from different viewpoints and a long, hard look at yourself in a full length mirror, you can grasp how the essential framework—the skeleton—supports the rest of the body. You can feel, as well as see, how one part is attached to another. By shifting your weight, bending or leaning to one side you can observe how the various sections stretch or contract. See how lines that are horizontal when the figure is standing erect—the line across the shoulders, the waistline and the hipline—assume quite acute angles in movement.

Study and draw the human figure by using a large mirror and,

In repose the muscles relax. Contrast this drawing by William Mulready with the standing nude on the opposite page, where the muscles of the leg and arm are tense as they take the weight of the stance.

whenever possible, a model. Draw from the nude and from clothed figures too. Observe the way in which different styles of clothing, made in different fabrics, cling to and hang from the body. Think again about what sort of drawing medium to use.

Just the same kind of enquiring observations should be applied to plants when you set out to draw them. If it is at all possible have available more than one specimen of the type of plant you are studying. This means that you can cut up one of them in order to comprehend its structure more completely, while another remains intact. Use a razor blade or very sharp craft knife for the cutting.

Plants are constructed upon a geometric symmetrical framework. In this way they resemble humans and other animals, with their symmetrical skeletons. Removing whole petals of a flower will enable you to see just what shape they really are. Often they are compressed or partly obliterated in the complete flower. A vertical cut across a flower head will reveal how the component parts form the shape—frequently far more complex than at first sight. (A magnifying glass might also be useful here).

Be thoughtful about the medium you choose for your plant drawings. For monochrome work use a tool that will give delicate, controlled lines. Harder pencils, fine pens or brushes are suitable. If you are working in colour be sure once again that the medium can be used in a delicate, subtle way. You'll need, especially for flower work, a coloured medium with the appropriate brilliance and 'living' quality. Experiment with coloured inks and water-soluble coloured pencils. These two types of materials are like watercolour paint, transparent, thus allowing the white of the paper to shine through. Consequently the colours have a quality nearer to that of flower petals than say, poster paint. Poster paint is thick and opaque. Petals painted with it will appear dull and heavy, lacking life. It's worthwhile trying out some different types of paper too. H.P. watercolour paper is eminently suited to coloured plant studies.

Try drawing a plant actual size. Select the view of it that you like best and arrange it so that the background immediately surrounding it is plain and uncluttered. If you are using a living cut specimen, as opposed to a dried one, it may be wise either to place it in water, or to wrap the end of the stem in some dampened tissue inside a small plastic bag. It takes some considerable time to draw flowers properly and you don't want to end up with just a limp stalk and a small pile of wilted petals.

If you are working in colour the area of the background immediately surrounding your specimen is important. The colour of the background is going to have an effect upon the colours of the plant itself. So don't unthinkingly draw the plant on your white paper as an isolated thing on a white background. You may match up a pink petal colour beautifully, but what might look a pale pink against the brown background of a

BLACKTHORN
CHIDDINGSTONE
KENT   1910
CRM   MMM

table-top will read as a much stronger pink against the white paper background. Interpret the background colour in your work too. This applies similarly in a monochrome drawing. The tonal relationship of plant to background must be carefully observed. Even if your plant specimen is lying on a white background; check to see in which ways that white background differs from the white drawing paper. Your plant may be influencing the background by causing shadows (if so, what colours are they?), or by reflecting its own local colour onto it.

In contrast, at least regarding scale, consider your approach towards drawing architecture. There is a rich source of subject matter here, ranging from the suburban house through to the ornate Gothic cathedral. Have a good look around your own local environment, possibly now with new awareness, to select some interesting views that will show you this diversity in different styles of buildings. In addition to their shapes look for variations in building materials. See how, for example, a wall made of marble contrasts with one in new brick; how does stark, new brick look against some older, mellow brickwork—and how are you going to portray that very difference in your drawing? Is it to do with the nature of the edges, the textures or the colour? How will you treat glass, modern cladding materials and wood? Look too at the way in which natural forms and elements are intermingled with the architecture. These will be figures and animals, trees, plants, water and on a broader scale, the sky and the terrain in which the buildings are set. Once again, consider how you will show these vastly differing qualities.

Having had some experience in observing and drawing you will now have used basic linear perspective construction. Walking around a town or village observe how the change in your viewpoint produces a dramatic alteration in the perspective lines. This is particularly noticeable if you climb some steps, stopping every so often to see how things do change. Why not make some drawings to record your observations? Take your cardboard viewfinder along to help you select an area to study. If you stand at the foot of the steps your horizon/eye level is going to be as high as you are tall. All the horizontal lines or edges of things that are not parallel to picture plane will, as always in perspective, appear to slope toward the vanishing point. (To reiterate briefly, those above the horizon/eye level slope downwards, those below upwards). As you are quite low down at the foot of the steps there is only a small area below your horizon/eye level and a large area above it. The top edges of any buildings that are directed, as it were, into the picture plane (edges where a wall meets a roof, for instance) will appear to slope downwards quite dramatically. Such angles can be seen to be getting less and less acute the nearer they get to the horizon/eye level. When they coincide with it they are horizontal; below it they start to slope upwards.

In fig.16, the artist Canaletto, in his eighteenth century pen and watercolour drawing, is viewing the scene standing on the same ground level as the other figures in the crowd. His viewpoint is to the right of the centre. The Venetian architecture is highly decorated and the piazza is full of detailed incidents, so that the whole picture looks extremely complicated. In spite of this, there is, underlying the entire scene, still the basic simple perspective construction. Note how any element that is repeated diminishes in size as it recedes from the viewer. This can be seen in the windows, the architectural decoration and the people.

Returning from the festivities of Venice to your own hometown, continue climbing up the steps and observe what has happened. The pavement or road, or whatever constituted the ground, formed a very small area of the composition when you were actually standing on it, has now greatly increased in size. You have moved upwards above the ground level and so your horizon/eye level is now much higher up. There is a great deal to see now below the horizon/eye level. Remember how a vast panorama stretches before you when you look out from a high tower. Up to the steps you may even be in a position where the

Fig. 16 Canaletto, pen and wash

line of a building that is made by the wall meeting the roof coincides with your eye level and appears as a horizontal. Perhaps you can go above it and see it as a line now appearing to slope upwards, away toward the vanishing point.

Canaletto's Venetian drawings show how architectural subjects can absorb an artist thoroughly, presenting him with endless vistas and perspectives. Venice has, of course, always held a fascination for painters with its wonderful contrasts of stone and water, permanence and shifting surfaces. In fact artists such as Guardi were far more sensitive to these contrasts than Canaletto, whose work conveys a great sense of mathematical precision and order. This is where his draughtsmanship comes into play most forcibly. It is certain that he made a consistent practice of drawing his verticals with a pencil and ruler, and he also used a technique called 'pin-pointing' mapping out distances.

Maintaining Observation

In drawing as, in fact, in any craft (or perhaps even any way of life) once one becomes fairly proficient one has to guard against complacency occurring. This can creep up in a most insidious way. Unfortunately some seemingly proficient drawings are nothing more than a collection of accomplished tricks. Once acquired these tricks lead the artist to cease looking at the subject being drawn. The subject no longer suggests how the drawing should be formed; the 'artistry' steps in and takes over. The artist has forgotten that the subject is there to supply information to him. The following is the sort of instance that can all too easily occur.

You are contentedly drawing out of doors, comfortably positioned in front of a most interesting view—a charming jetty, boats and some

Pen, ink and wash drawing by Giovanni Piranesi.

113

cottages, under a partly clouded sky. The temperature is just right, the breeze so slight that it refreshes without irritating. What a perfect way to spend an afternoon. You have previously found yourself enjoying quite a measure of success when drawing skies. This pleases you particularly as you found the sky such a problem when you first took up drawing as a hobby. You've developed an effective method of first applying light shading as a tone, made up of evenly sloping parallel strokes, to represent the clear blue areas. You then delicately outline the cloud shapes with a hard pencil. One or two people have, in fact, commented favourably on your clever treatment of the sky.

So, off you go again this afternoon—first the sensitive shading (careful, even sloping lines) leading up to the outlining of the clouds.

From Paysages Urbains, *Stanley Hayter, dry-point engraving.*

But stop a minute! Do you realize that apart from the first moment when you arrived at this place to select which view you would draw you haven't looked at the sky at all? It has registered in your mind—"Ah yes, sky with clouds"—and almost like a machine your hand has automatically started to produce the much-admired cloud rendering.

If this description rings an uncomfortable bell—take yourself in hand. Concentrate upon that particular subject or technique about which you were becoming so complacent. Try these three suggested remedies. First, deliberately set about doing drawings with a particular emphasis on the beastly subject. Secondly, use a material or a combination of materials new to you. This, in a way, forces you back nearer to the innocent stage of the beginner. Try, for example, working in a way that is quite the reverse to your normal technique. If you generally use a dark pen or pencil line on white paper try out a white line drawing on black scraperboard; or blacken your paper first with charcoal and draw into it with whites and greys made with an eraser. Finally, track down, either via museums or books from your local library, examples of the work of artists who have successfully handled your particular *bete noire*. In the case of skies, for instance, John Constable's sketches and paintings cannot fail to inspire you. J.M.W. Turner, another English painter who lived from 1775 to 1851, was also deeply interested in this nebulous subject.

Studying the work of other artists and seeing how they have approached the many and varied problems of drawing is invaluable to you. Being able to examine the original work in a museum or art gallery is, of course, best of all. Do, however, also look at reproductions in

Above. This engraving is taken from Sebastiano Serlio's Second Book of Perspective *and is a design for a stage back drop.*

Below. Boulevard, *Pierre Bonnard, lithograph.*

Right. Relativity, *M. C. Escher,*
lithograph.
Far right. System of Iconography;
plug, mouse, good humour
bar, switches and lipstick,
Claes Oldenburg, pencil. Many artists
rely on their imagination for
subject matter, assembling the
objects and scenes of everyday life
in unreal situations.

books, especially in the more expensively produced volumes, some of which should be available in your library. The higher the quality of the reproduction, the closer it will resemble the original. While you are looking at these works, remember the different aspects that were discussed in the general theme of 'the grammar' of drawing. See what diverse poetry this grammar can produce.

Feedback from other people who are also engaged in painting or drawing is important to you. Discussion around a shared and loved subject inevitably activates ideas. Hearing new points of view can lead you into previously unexplored and unimagined territories of drawing. Working entirely alone, especially in the early stages, is not really a good idea. You need the stimulus of conversation and argument with like-minded people. Unless they too are studying the subject, the reactions

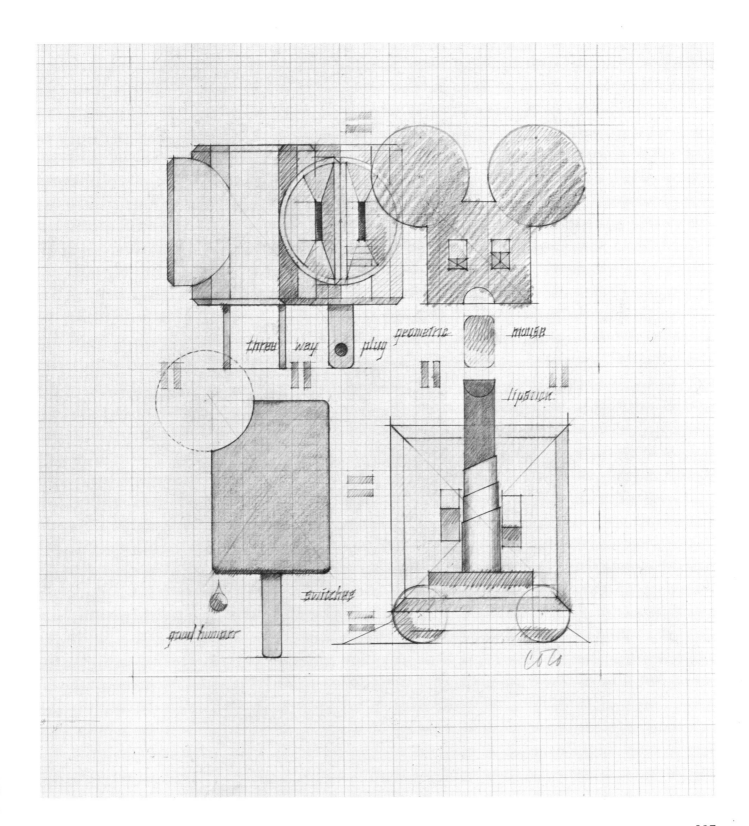

three way   plug   geometric   mouse

lipstick

switches

good humor

This *Arthur Rackham illustration is from the* Ring of Nibelung *by Richard Wagner. Myths and fairy tales offer great scope for imaginative drawing. Presented with a narrative, it is left to the artist to create a fanciful world peopled by magical beings.*

of your family and friends to your work, however well-intentioned, will give you no constructive criticism. Consider the idea of attending a part-time class or joining a local art group or club. The fees are generally reasonable. Such an organization may well be able to offer you a number of advantages—qualified tuition, ample space in which to work, professional models, possible lectures and museum visits and an atmosphere conducive to quiet study. You will be able to benefit from (and also

Cartoons, such as this one by Ray Lowry, are the most obvious example of how a drawing is able instantly to convey a message. Most often the cartoon is humourous, but its success always relies on well-observed expression portrayed in an economical manner.

contribute toward) the helpful criticism and suggestions of your colleagues, and compare your progress to that of others.

Imaginative drawing

When drawing from the imagination, or from your memory bank of accumulated visual information, all the same 'grammar guidelines' discussed earlier still apply. Indeed, and this is important, if you lack the technical understanding of how the component parts of a drawing are assembled into the final whole you will never be able to give shape to your image, no matter how exotic and exciting the pictures may be inside your head. Planning the composition is still just as important in a work drawn from the imagination. Consider carefully how the elements of the drawing are to be arranged. Is the desired effect going to be achieved with a cluttered, closely filled, highly detailed picture in which the observer is led along all sorts of mysterious and possibly disturbing paths, or is an air of tranquility, an enviable dreamland, to be suggested by carefully placed items isolated in space.

If you feel you would like to try some kind of imaginative drawing but you just can't think how to set about it, here are a few suggestions that may help you to get going. The process is rather like recalling the balmy days of childhood, when your own personal idiosyncratic brand of logic linked one thing with another, quite regardless of the so-called rational world. A similar state seems to prevail in dreams.

Take a container that you have in the house—a vase, a jug, a bottle or a box. What might its contents be? Ordinarily the bottle holds, say, cooking oil. Maybe the box contains a motley collection of paper clips, used stamps, rubber bands and odd buttons. Supposing the normal state of things was entirely changed. The box became full of little people, all pushing and shoving to open the lid and climb out and escape, or the bottle was knocked over onto its side. Instead of cooking oil spilling out, a curious misty vapour swirled out from its neck; rather like Aladdin's lamp, the vapour eddied upwards and transformed itself into elegant oriental bird shapes. The birds finally took flight, and with a great flapping, a bizarre, screeching, brilliantly coloured flock rose into the sky.

Here is another idea that may spark off ideas for an imaginative composition. Place two seemingly unrelated objects together—selected at random—perhaps a rose and a rotary beater. How can these two things be linked together? Think of all the ways in which they could— write your thoughts down if it helps to stimulate the imagination. Beaten roses, pink, creamy and with a delicate froth, to which one added ingredients to make a floral cake? (Do the thorns survive the mixing process and remain intact in the cake?) Alternatively, the invasive living plant taking over the inanimate metal machine, stifling

it with relentless growth? Other emotive associated thoughts suggest themselves when the concept of rose and beater is considered. There are many literary illusions to the rose—rosy dawn; rose pink; the rose thorn pricks and flesh and draws blood—the beater; the victorious and so on. Following a train of thought like this often leads to final concepts that are far removed from the original source of stimulus, but this sort of creative thinking shows that you are aware of possibilities and not restricted by what you actually see.

Vision de Tondal, *Hieronymous Bosch, oil. This 15th century Dutch artist is noted for his juxtaposition of the realistic and fantastic.* (*fig. 19*)

On another track, are there visible similarities between the two objects? Does the flower head, with its concentric arrangement of petals at the end of a stalk rather resemble the heads of the beaters? Do the leaves jutting out at right angles to the stalk look somewhat like the cranking handle on the side of the beater? Perhaps there are certain similarities in design, but in quality the two articles are poles apart. How, in your drawing, do you explain the dead hardness of the metal in contrast to the living plant?

This is only the merest taste of how you might begain to approach imaginative drawing. If the subject appeals to you, do follow it up in books on Dada and Surrealism. These were two artistic movements, starting with Dada in 1915, which sought to shake free from the artistic conventions of the time. However, the surrealist, dream-like approach has been present in literature and the visual arts for centuries. Hieronymus Bosch (1450-1516), for instance, portrayed the most nightmarish creatures in his paintings (see fig. 19); many old fairy tales are full of surrealist allusions. What Shakespeare says of the poet could just as well apply to the artist:

> " . . . . as imagination bodies forth
> The forms of things unknown, the poet's pen
> Turns them to shapes, and gives to airy nothing
> A local habitation and a name."

The Finished Drawing

Try to be reasonably methodical about the way in which you keep your drawings. As you progress you will produce more and more, and proper storage is essential. Paper is a vulnerable material and should be protected from damage, dust and dirt. It is wise to invest in a portfolio. These are available in several sizes and are made of stout, covered cardboard. The portfolio has inner flaps so, when it is closed, the drawings inside are protected on all four edges. The whole thing fastens with ribbon tapes. Portfolios vary in quality and price. Some have reinforced corners for extra protection. A more expensive type is the folio case. This, generally in leather-look plastic, has a zipper or a flap and is like a giant, flat briefcase. Obviously, these are more expensive than the cardboard portfolios but they are useful if you have to travel a lot with your work.

Store your drawings flat and never roll a drawing except inside a strong cardboard tube. This is a good way to send them through the mail. A roll of paper alone, even just being carried home after a day's drawing outdoors, can all too easily get squashed, resulting in permanent creases down the drawing. Charcoal, pastel and similar kinds of drawing, although they have been treated with fixative, are still a little inclined to smudge. Lay a sheet of thin paper over each drawing in the portfolio. Use tissue, tracing or layout paper for this.

Mounting drawings

A cardboard mount around a drawing performs the same function as the viewfinder that you use when actually making a drawing. It isolates the picture from the surroundings, so that it may be seen free from interference. You can simply stick a drawing onto a sheet of mounting board but the best way of presenting a drawing is to use a window mount. The picture is recessed behind a flat surround, or frame, of cardboard. For this you will need two pieces of cardboard. One piece goes behind the drawing to act as a support. This can be a cheaper, thinnish type of board: it's not going to be on view, serving only to protect the back of the drawing. However, especially if your drawing is on thin paper, choose a white backing as a colour might show through. The other

Fig. 1 The colour you choose for a picture mount must be carefully considered. These three examples show the effects produced by a dark, light and brightly coloured border around the same drawing. The brown mount tends to subdue the colours, the blue to highlight them and the cream serves no purpose at all.

piece of cardboard forms the flat frame shape. Here the quality should be well considered. Mounting board, as this second type of cardboard is called, can be bought at an art shop or a stationers. They will also stock the thinner type of board. Mounting board is available in several different thicknesses and in a range of colours.

You will also require some masking tape, a craft knife (with a good sharp blade), a metal ruler and a surface on which to cut. This could be a piece of heavy cardboard or a sheet of glass. Masking tape is the best type of adhesive tape here, and for a variety of similar jobs. Should you want to lift it off, you can do so without its spoiling the surface of the cardboard or paper. Also it does not become sticky on the back as do some types of transparent adhesive tapes after a period of time.

Be sure when mounting drawings that everything is absolutely clean— the surfaces on which you are working and your own hands. It's so easy to get unfortunate finger marks on a piece of pristine white board, and so difficult to remove them without trace. Keep some clean white paper handy (perhaps a few sheets of typing paper). These will be useful to place between the work and your hand when you need to press down, as when sticking two layers together.

Deciding how big the mount should be and what colour is best brings your judgement of composition into play again. A great deal depends upon the kind of drawing being mounted; whether it is a strong, heavy image or a very delicate one. As a general rule, be generous with the mount. A narrow edging just looks thoughtless. The colour and tone of the mounting board should be carefully selected in relation to the drawing. The illustration in fig. 1 shows the completely different effect on a picture (which has a light background and lightweight colouring) that a dark toned, a light toned and a strong coloured mount produce. Take your drawing along to the art shop so that you can see how it looks against the various coloured mounting boards.

The mount should be of similar proportion to the drawing, larger by the amount of margin you have chosen. If you place a picture exactly in the centre of a mount, it will, curiously enough, look as if it's too low. Always make the lower margin a little wider than the top one to compensate for this optical illusion. The two side margins will be the same width as each other.

Before you cut the mounting board down to the required size, do some practice cutting, just to get the hang of it. Mark out the outer dimensions of the finished mount and then you'll know how much cardboard you have got to spare for practising. Lay the board on the cutting surface. Press down on the metal ruler and cut slowly and firmly running the knife against the ruler's edge. Don't use anything but a metal ruler. Plastic or wooden ones are bound to get cut. If yours is a bevel-edged ruler, you can try cutting a bevel, that is, making your cut at an angle. This adds an air of quality to the mount. The edges of the window will slope in toward the drawing. To cut a bevel, slope your

Fig. 2 Lightly trace around the window opening onto the backing.
Fig. 3 Tape the drawing in position.
Fig. 4 Then tape the window mount in place over the drawing.
Fig. 5 Finally attach the backing to the window mount.

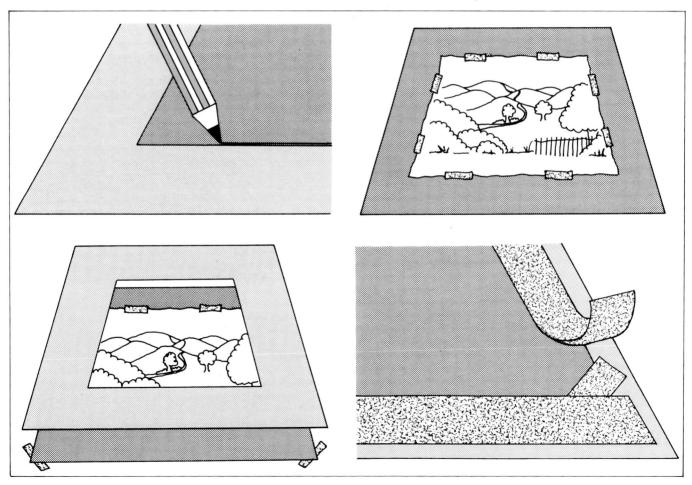

knife blade to rest against the edge of the ruler and keep it at that angle throughout the cut. Whether cutting out a straight or a bevelled mount, practise doing a few corners too.

A window mount slightly overlaps the drawing by a minimum of 3mm ($\frac{1}{8}$in) all the way around. When you measure out the area that is to be cut away, do not forget to allow for this overlap. It makes each margin 3mm ($\frac{1}{8}$in) wider on the cardboard. Lightly pencil in the window area on the front face of the mounting board. Carefully cut around it and remove that central section. Cut the backing card down so that it is 1cm ($\frac{1}{2}$in) smaller all around than the mounting board. Place it on the table and centre the mounting board on top of it. Now, very lightly and carefully, making sure you don't mark the window edges, pencil through the cut-out window onto the backing card to show the cut-out area (fig. 2). Lift the mounting board away. You can now position the drawing on this lightly pencilled shape. It should overlap the shape by at least 3mm ($\frac{1}{8}$in) on all sides. Fasten the drawing down to the backing card with short lengths of masking tape. Make sure you arrange these so that they protrude over the drawing by no more than 3mm ($\frac{1}{8}$in). Use short lengths of masking tape rather than continuous long pieces. They are easier to handle (fig. 3).

Having fixed the drawing to the backing board, place four short pieces of masking tape at the outer corners of the backing card, attached to the back of it and sticking out just a little, with the sticky side uppermost. Lower the window mount into position over the drawing (fig. 4). Press the outer corners down, enough to make contact with the pieces of masking tape on the backing card. Gently lift the whole thing, turn it over and place face down. Now fasten the backing card securely to the back of the mount with more lengths of masking tape (fig. 5). The window mount is then complete. Should you wish to remount the drawing at a later date or want to store it unmounted you can easily remove this type of mount without causing any damage.

A further refinement which may be added to the window mount is to rule a line or lines around the aperture. A felt pen is useful here as it gives a line of even thickness.

Framing

If you wish to display a drawing on the wall or you are entering one for an exhibition, framing is essential. Being vulnerable, a drawing needs the protection of glass. The frame should harmonize with the drawing and the mount. A frame-maker or a wood supplier will show you a selection of different frame mouldings. If you are a competent carpenter, by all means make your own frames. The corners need to be mitred. Otherwise, as making a traditional wooden frame is quite a skilled job, use the services of a professional framer.

Left. Frames should be chosen in accordance with the decor of the room. Wooden and gilt frames are well-suited to this traditional setting.

As with the mount, be selective in your choice of frame. Don't choose one that is going to dominate the drawing because it is too thick and heavy, elaborately decorated or too strong in colour.

It is advisable to ask a frame-maker to use acid-free materials when he frames your drawing. A sheet of board is used at the back of the picture frame, and some types of board contain chemicals which can cause the paper of your drawing to discolour. Also, consider the use of non-reflecting glass. It is more expensive, so ask to see some examples before making your decision.

There are several do-it-yourself framing kits on the market. Most of these have fairly plain mouldings in wood, aluminium or plastic. They are supplied complete with backing board and glass. The wooden frames may be left as natural wood or painted, waxed or varnished. These kits are quite easy to assemble. Their only disadvantage is that they are available only in certain set sizes, which of course, may not fit your particular purpose.

Below. Modern aluminium frames can look very attractive, and are widely available in kit form. Unfortunately the range of sizes is rather limited.

Index